time for Her

Printed in Australia
Cover and internal design by Shawline Publishing Group Pty Ltd
First Printing: August 2023

Shawline Publishing Group Pty Ltd
www.shawlinepublishing.com.au

Paperback ISBN 978-1-9229-9384-7
Ebook ISBN 978-1-9229-9390-8

Distributed by Shawline Distribution and Lightning Source Global

 A catalogue record for this
work is available from the
National Library of Australia

More great Shawline titles can be found by scanning the QR code below.
New titles also available through Books@Home Pty Ltd.
Subscribe today at www.booksathome.com.au or scan the QR code below.

A MEMOIR OF TRUE ROMANCE

time for Her

MITCH LARSSON

For P.

First thanks must go to Dr Liz Monument my fabulous editor. Your seemingly effortless talent helped me take what I thought was a pretty decent manuscript to the next level and it could not have become what it is without your brilliant mind.

To the lovely Ms B - thank you not only for helping me with the first few edits and marketing advice, but also for your positive energy your unwavering belief in me and what I do. And for helping me believe in myself. You've been my inspiration, my cheerleader and my confidant since we first met all those years ago. You've seen me absolutely flying, and you've seen me come crashing down in a blubbering mess and I adore you for that.

To my amazing friend Germain - you somehow managed to find the time to read through my manuscript in its infancy despite your incredibly hectic schedule zipping around the globe as a cinematic genius, and I am incredibly grateful for that. As teenagers, and now as men, I feel we've both understood and embraced each other's crazy ways without judgement. You truly are a lifelong friend, Kid.

Finally, to my beloved "Sam" – I hope somehow, somewhere, you'll be able to understand the profound impact you've had on my life. Even after all this time, there's rarely a day I don't think about you and the amazing times we had together. You've left a painful, but beautiful hole in my heart that I will always cherish.

Preface

The following memoir is a personal account based on my own recollections and experiences. Whilst I have made every effort to ensure its accuracy and authenticity, memories are subjective by nature and are influenced by the passage of time – not to mention decades of partying and substance abuse. Names, locations and specific details have been altered or omitted to protect the privacy and identities of every individual involved. The events and conversations portrayed in this memoir are my interpretations and reflections, and I ask you, my dear reader, to approach them with an open mind and to understand that they may differ from the perspectives of others. This memoir is not intended to offend or defame anyone, but rather to share my unique journey, and the lessons I've learned along the way. In a similar vein, if you are reading this as someone who has met me professionally, please know that I have not forgotten the time we shared together. On the contrary, the intimacy involved in this profession makes it very difficult to forget, so please know that any omissions I have made in this memoir are for the sake of brevity.

Chapter 1 — The Leap

When I first saw Facebook in the late 2000s, I clearly remember thinking how dangerous it could become and how amazing it was that people willingly shared so much of themselves for free. I had no desire to tell the world, 'What's on my mind?' as Facebook asked me to. I had no need to broadcast every thought I had, every meal I ate or any sorrow I pretended I was feeling. When you're selling something, however, and especially when that something is *you*, a social media presence is vital. And my potential customers, more than anyone, needed reassurance that if they gave me their hard-earned dollars, I would provide them with the outcome they desired; perhaps even their wildest dreams.

Because my service was sex.

I signed up to Twitter in the early days of my new career, on the advice of a sex worker colleague. I'd churn out random tweets designed to reassure my growing audience that I was a sexy and trustworthy guy. Dignity and security are primary concerns for the women I see. Some of them have escaped from abusive relationships; others are lonely and want the safety net of knowing they can go out for a dinner-date, but won't end up with a creep from one of the various dating apps. It's a financial transaction, yes, but it's also so much more than that. My services have been everything from straight-out fun or a much-needed confidence boost to reconnecting lost, tired or scared women with a sense of themselves they haven't had in years.

All roles grow and my budding career was no exception. But as the months rolled on, I became more entangled in the lives of the women who booked me. I tuned in to their unique situations, listened to their confided secrets, absorbed their needs and desires, and eventually, (and perhaps inevitably) the line between personal and professional began to blur. Finally, on one particularly lonely and dark day, I reached out on social media to do something more than tell people I was an honest, caring and safe playmate. I suppose it was a cry in the dark: the need to be heard, or maybe even a way to unburden myself – and it was about Sam. Here's the message I posted on Twitter:

I have a regular client who is suffering from early-onset Alzheimer's disease and she's only forty-six. She said she has about five years to live and is aware that she is declining rapidly. She has chosen me to be her companion in the last years of her life, as dating is pointless to her. To say I'm honoured is a vast understatement. She has a carer and supportive friends but an unsupportive ex-husband, and two young kids. She understandably needs sexual release but it's become far more.

She talks of making videos of us so she can remember me for as long as possible and I completely die inside. She knows she will never live to see her children become adults and the hopelessness of her situation becomes overwhelming.

I saw her last night and didn't want to stop holding her. The amount of time she books me for becomes irrelevant. I want to be everything and nothing to her at the same time. I guess I'm not really looking for advice as much as a few virtual hugs. I honestly can't stop crying.

I was blown away by the compassion I was shown, and it helped me to understand that none of us work or live in a bubble and that our circumstances can change in the blink of an eye.

I'm Mitch Larsson, and this is my story.

***

I'd always been flirtatious. By choosing sex work as a career, I was able to harness what I saw as a strength and turn it into a job that put a roof over my head, paid my bills, helped support my son, and yes, even paid my taxes. When women looked at the images of the Mitch Larsson persona I'd created, however, with the work-out body, the well-cut suit and the descriptive spiel that invited them to 'feel cared for and loved in the most genuine, non-judgmental way possible', adjectives mattered. And not the ones you would think. Yes, one needed to look good in this industry, but it was also much, much more important to be seen as safe. The most chiseled abs in the world won't get you booked if you aren't trustworthy and kind.

Mitch definitely didn't come cheap, but investing in your own safety, pleasure and self-worth wasn't meant to be. He was a man who respected, celebrated and adored women. Mitch was the guy that just about every woman wanted at some stage in their lives and in lots of ways, he was the man I always wanted to be. But Dan – the real me – came as part of the package, too, and I couldn't be one man without being true to the other...

I was always a bit of a fuck-up, really. I know, in many ways, that's how my family saw me too. Or, as my parents more tenderly liked to put it sometimes, I was 'always interesting'.

Dan the Drifter.

Dan the Dabbler.

Dan the Dreamer.

But I was also Dan the Dad. Dan the Married Guy Who Became

Separated and Single. And then finally, Dan the Former Lawyer Turned Escort.

I know it wasn't a 'normal' career trajectory, but ever since I received my first official bipolar diagnosis in my twenties, I've questioned what normal is anyway. For me, it was normal to think of a wildly ambitious goal for myself and wonder why it couldn't happen then and there. It was normal to focus every molecule of my energy single-mindedly on trying to make an ambitious idea materialise, at all costs, but then just as normal to feel like it was very suddenly too hard or, more accurately, too boring. It was also normal for me to dump that plan, wonder what the hell I'd done with my life, and then dream of a new, completely different plan. The 2.3 kid, 9 to 5 white-collar life, to me, sounded like absolute torture.

I'd always had the feeling that I wanted to try everything. A different career, a different adrenaline rush, a different sexual partner. I was a signed-up subscriber to the 'You Only Live Once' philosophy and for my wife at the time, that meant dealing with the revelation that I was thinking about other women after nine years of faithful marriage. I found it very difficult to hide my emotions at the best of times and after many turbulent months, it just had to come out. For me, being part of a married couple was something that felt like everything was fine and 'right' until it wasn't. It's a cliché, really. I know.

I'd been working out a hell of a lot to reshape my middle-aged body into something I thought was attractive. I wasn't happy, but I was strong and healthy. I wanted to be a superhero for my son, but I also wanted to feel sexy and alive and all the other textbook things people want to feel when they become unhappy with the decisions they've made and the person they've become. The trouble began when I started flirting with one of the mothers from my boy's day-care centre. After a while, this spilled over into sexy text messages, and my wandering mind was eventually exposed when my wife checked my phone. Like a complete bastard, my first reaction was to blame her for invading my privacy. It wasn't her fault in the slightest, and I quickly realised that my anger was actually misguided shame.

It was never a physical affair, but the easy intimacy we were sharing in those words and emojis may as well have been dick pics and declarations of undying love because, from my wife's perspective, it was a betrayal. She was right, but acknowledging that didn't make it any better and it didn't stop me wondering how we'd arrived at a juncture that so many couples before us had reached. Neither did it help me understand which way we were supposed to turn. In nine years of faithful marriage, until that very point – and in the long-term relationships I'd had before her, I'd never been a cheater and had always despised such men with a passion.

Yet, there we were.

Like the couples you read about in magazines or self-help books, with one partner complaining about losing touch with their sexuality and spontaneity and the other one feeling like life was busy enough as it was, with no time or inclination to lose touch with anything. It had dawned on me – and far too late – that the marriage vow of being with only one woman was part of an unsettling resentment that was churning me up. I felt like I'd lost my freedom but, like so many mid-life crisis-riddled men before me, I couldn't see clearly enough to know that what I was actually looking for was a sense of purpose.

When my wife read those text messages, my reaction was to feel violated but, really, it was a defensive distraction from a much deeper issue. So, we talked about it and, together, we tossed up the possibility of opening our marriage up. Actually, to clarify, it was me. I tossed it up – as more men seem to be doing these days. Did she really want to? Probably not, but after thinking carefully about it for a while and reading of others' experiences, she agreed to do what many other women have done before her and sanctioned my quest for sexual exploration with people who weren't her.

My sexual appetite had always been voracious. Sex, for me, was an all-consuming multi-sensory pleasure that was addictive and energising and, I must admit, I became pretty excited.

After the conversation about opening our marriage up to other people, I tried out Tinder and didn't pull any punches with my profile. I made it clear that I wasn't looking for long-term, as I already had that, but that I was there in the search to learn how to be the best lover I could possibly be. From my perspective, it was true. I hadn't been with anyone new for almost a decade and I wanted to test my abilities. I'd already graduated from law school, but now I was presented with a new type of education I was very happy to enrol in. For the women reading the online description of me, it had its own attraction, because it told them that I was a guy who was happy to help them discover their own sexual epiphanies as well. I was a guy who wanted to learn how to bring them joy – physically, at least. And to my surprise, quite a few chose me and swiped right. In the back of my mind, though, my Tinder foray had the potential to be something more, and I viewed it as a kind of apprenticeship, where I imagined myself clocking on to study at the coal-face of female desire.

The woman I'd had my text affair with had opened another door as well. She once commented on how connected I was to my sexuality and wondered if I'd ever been a stripper or an escort before.

An escort?

I suppose most people might hear someone ask that and feel kind of amused by the notion, then let the comment go just as quickly but, for me, it became a concept that started occupying my thoughts. I'd worked my way through a succession of career attempts already, but maybe this time I'd find what I was really looking for. I'd left one steady job after another over many years and returned to university to get my law degree. That gamble led to some volunteer work with a community legal service before I accepted a job at a small legal practice in country NSW. Then, when we fell pregnant, the seemingly obvious decision – who was to be our son's primary caregiver – was made to enable my wife to return to her own more established and far more lucrative career in medicine.

After four years of changing nappies and mind-numbing playground visits, I was left with the feeling of being far too removed from legal practice despite all my hard work, and that realisation became the catalyst to recreate myself as the professional photographer I'd dreamed of becoming since I was a child. But, aside from an attempt to specialise in the fitness industry aspect of the commercial photography world, that hadn't really worked out either. Contributing to the family coffers through the lens of my camera was a constantly frustrating hustle from one low-paying gig to another and at forty-one, I didn't want to go back to the law, even though my all-too-brief dalliance with it probably gave my parents a taste of what it looked like to have a son who was stable, ambitious and ready to function in regular society.

So, one morning I woke up after a particularly long and restless night, and I decided to take the plunge. I put the idea of getting paid to have sex with women for a living to my wife, and when I asked her if it was wrong, to my amazement, she only had one question:

'Is it wrong that I don't think that's wrong?'

Was she really happy about it or was she just loosening the reins in an attempt to hold onto a marriage with a frustrated (and frustrating) husband? From where I stood, already plotting my take-over of the world of male escorts, it appeared she was genuinely by my side and seemed to be even just a bit titillated at the idea of me hawking my sexual wares as a career path.

For a conservative professional, who'd grown up in an affluent part of Sydney and followed the conventional path of ticking off the desirable list of education, ambition, marriage and family,

I believe that my proposal was intriguing to her on some level. Or possibly she saw it as a paid extension of the open marriage she'd only just managed to accept. I was sure a lot of it was out of love and care for me too, though. Mental health was a tightrope I'd struggled to balance on for years. I had looked for new ways to escape and push the boundaries of Dan throughout my life, and now I had permission to create an alternate version of me, an alternate reality where I could see whether living someone else's life would make me happier than living my own. Both of us were curious about where it might take us, but neither of us, naively, expected it to take such a toll on our relationship.

I chose the name Mitch, after Mitch Rapp, the protagonist in a favourite book series of mine by Vince Flynn. In the novels, he's an arse-kicking, bullet-proof assassin, and to form my own new identity, I added a surname that I envisaged as a kind of cool, classy Nordic *nom de plume*. Larsson. Mitch Larsson.

On paper, Mitch presented as more of an exhibitionist than Dan. He was happy to talk openly about sex and his love of it, which is something I'd spent my adulthood trying to silence. But honestly, there wasn't much difference between Dan and Mitch and because I was a guy who was straight down the line and didn't handle pretense for too long, it usually didn't take long before my clients saw right through my Mitch visage. I knew of no other way.

I've spoken to a lot of female sex workers, and for many of them, protecting their real lives from their sex worker identity is something they are meticulous about. They have their 'work name' and they stick to it. I came to fully understand why very quickly after I began when one of my early clients became downright nasty when I didn't reply to her many messages. It's much easier reading hateful messages directed at someone else so I was glad Mitch was around. Having a few female admirers push the boundaries is, at most, unpleasant for us guys, but for the girls in the industry, things can often get scary – and in some cases, much, much worse. I therefore always stuck to being called Mitch for a first booking, but once I felt safe I preferred to use my real name because the truth was that if I tried to embrace Mitch as a character, I would feel like I was putting on a costume. And I felt deceptive. As Mitch, those were the moments when I looked in on myself as if I was watching a scene in a movie, and it was in those moments I lost connection to my partner's body. In (im)practical terms, I could also lose my erection as a result. I was breaking the mould of what a detached escort was meant to be, and I knew it meant I was crossing a line and giving myself another tightrope to criss-cross my other father/husband balancing act.

I've tried performative sex (more about that later) and, although I'd have to employ it as a skill every now and then with a client I didn't feel a true connection with, the reality was that I had to feel an actual *affection* and form of love, in order to make love. I had to feel that in a relationship and I had to feel that with a client, even if it was just a one-off three-hour booking. Playing a part didn't work for me, and it was often to my detriment.

I know some of the other guys out there are capable of walking into a job, doing the deed and walking out. But that wasn't me. Dan might've been part Mitch, but Mitch was more parts Dan.

And that was about to cause problems.

Chapter 2 – Number One

We talked about our open marriage, my Tinder dalliance, and the launch of myself as a sex worker. But, in between, I also wished for my wife to have the same freedom I was asking for in my own life. I knew that if I was proposing an arrangement that would permit me to sleep with other women, it had to be equal, and so I told my wife that if she wanted to explore her sexuality with other people as well, it was something that would be fine with me. It didn't sit particularly well with me, but it was important that I kept my end of the deal. The physical aspect of her being with someone else bothered me, but it was more than that. I think a lot of it had to do with my competitive nature. I wanted my wife to live life to the fullest and to be happy, but the idea of another man pleasing her more than I could really affected me. Conceptually, however, it was exciting, and I still remember that time in our marriage as a place that felt engaging and alive. Talking about it became a type of foreplay for us and, although she never acted on it, I made sure that it was something she felt truly felt open to – and not just something she was saying to keep us together. It was the least I could do.

Once the decision to become a male escort was made, the research to find the most trustworthy, top-ranking directory to sign up to was something we both dug into. My wife's continuing support amazed me. I should also describe her as incredibly patient, as well, because if she was hoping that I'd grow out of it eventually, she didn't show it. Would I have acted the same way if my own partner had approached me about her desire to have sex with other people – and then hit me again with the idea of becoming a paid, professional sex worker? I guess I'll never know, but what I do know is that she is definitely one of the most amazing women I'll ever meet, and I'll always be sorry for the pain I caused her by flirting with that mum from my son's playgroup.

The next steps were about getting down to business. My own ideas about how to create enticing profile pics and a bio were informed by looking at the way the other guys presented themselves on various sites, and then by figuring out what I could do to more accurately reflect the type of man I was – as well as the service I believed I could provide. I did some research on Reddit forums, where I read tales from women revealing their good (and awful) experiences with male escorts, and this also helped – mainly because it confirmed what I already knew about what women probably *didn't* want from a trusted companion-for-hire. One surprised young lady spoke of opening her door to a man who looked nothing like the pictures she'd seen. Not even close. Another complained that her date spent most of the time in the bathroom on his phone, drank copious amounts of booze and fell asleep. The true 'Boyfriend Experience', it would seem.

Having professional camera equipment at my disposal was very handy, and my wife helped me take the photos for the site. She also took on the unofficial stylist role to help me settle on what would be most attractive for the audience I was pitching to. Some shots were of my body, oiled and partially undressed; others were more akin to a guy in an editorial spread, advertising designer watches. My lovely wife was never as sexual as I was but suddenly there was a new spark, and we suddenly found ourselves loving each other in new ways – a respite from the grind of being parents to a pre-school kid, which gave us fresh hope.

She proofread the bio I wrote, and when I got my first legitimate enquiry shortly afterwards, she seemed almost as excited as I was. She advised me on grooming matters and helped me choose an outfit that was all casual sophistication, with pale chinos, a well-cut t-shirt and a dark blazer. I'd primped and preened myself to the nth degree and applied the Mitch armour of some scented moisturiser (a great, inoffensive aftershave substitute by the way) and stocked up on breath mints. After we put our son to bed for the night, I kissed her goodbye and left for my Saturday night shift at an address more than an hour away on the Mornington Peninsula.

I was leaving our family home as a husband and father, then mentally shifted my mindset into what would become 'Mitch-mode'. This meant shifting away from my standard reality to think of myself as a successful, confident and single guy going out into the world, getting ready to please a woman. I was stepping out into the unknown with no idea who I was about to see, with the understanding that I would have sex with them. And, believe me, that last part changed everything. As I cruised along the freeway, mindlessly taking note as the distance to my destination grew less and less on the GPS, I could only imagine what my wife was thinking as she moved around our house. Maybe she was tucking our son in again or perhaps she was just sitting on the couch watching her beloved home renovation shows. Each thought elicited a sharp and extremely disconcerting pang of guilt so to clear my mind, I cracked the window open a little to let the warm summer's air in and pumped up some Eminem to try and wipe the thoughts of my beautiful little family from my mind.

I was nervous.

There was no denying that.

But when I pulled up to the address I'd been given – a low-brow, two-level courtyard motel in a slightly rougher end of town – and knocked on the door to find my first-ever client visibly shaking with nerves, I felt my instincts take over. She was thirty years old, and it was her friends who had originally contacted me on her behalf. Together, they'd all chipped in to buy me as a present to help her get back on the proverbial bike after a bad relationship break-up. She wore jeans with a white blouse, had straight brown hair that fell just past her shoulders and she had some fairly bad acne scars, but she was still quite beautiful. Judging by the empty cans I could see on the table in that small motel room, she had clearly been calming her nerves with pre-mixed bourbon and coke. I could smell cigarettes but could tell by her tight, youthful body that she looked after herself and I immediately became excited for what might follow. There was a gentle, kind beauty to her, despite the edge her anxiousness had given her, and when I invited her to come over for a hug and I wrapped my arms around her, I could feel her bury her head in my chest as if an unseen layer of tension was beginning to dissipate. We stayed that way for a while, just holding each other with me stroking her hair until finally, I asked if she would like me to kiss her.

'Oh, okay...' Her voice was barely a squeak but again, as our lips touched, I felt another release of tension as her body melted into mine while our excitement grew.

As in all intimate situations, consent is critical, but as a male escort for women, I felt an extra layer of care was needed. If I sensed any doubt or concern, I felt compelled to clearly determine whether it was okay to proceed. I don't know what rule book I was reading from on that particular night, but everything I said and did just seemed to come naturally to me and after more kissing, I asked if she felt like taking off my shirt. I'd already taken a moment to set up the Bluetooth speaker I learnt to bring with me to all my bookings to help with a background soundtrack, and her reply was a little louder this time as the music I'd chosen pulsed around us.

'Yeah, that'd be awesome.'

From there, everything happened pretty quickly. We moved

over to the bed, covered by the thin, overly starched and rigid sheets one would expect from such an establishment and shifted from one position to another in a fairly standard but still mutually exciting exploration of each other's bodies. Her story was one I've now come to know verbatim. She'd been dating a guy since her early twenties and was looking to find herself again after he broke her heart by sleeping with another girl. That had been quite a few months prior, but the pain persisted and made her reluctant to jump straight back into the dating scene. Her self-esteem had taken a huge hit, so now she was looking to take control over what she wanted sexually and who she wanted to share herself with. She longed for intimacy, but without the initial stress of hooking up with a random stranger online. Well not yet, anyway – and it was clear that I was there to help with her transition, even if it was with her friends' help.

Since then, I've come to realise that this is what I seemed to offer, whether I was helping my clients get over the loss of a connection with someone else or possibly the loss of their sense of self. It was often heavy stuff that took time and wasn't conducive to clock-watching, so as a result, I would often go well and truly over my allotted time. There was no running out the door with my money on the sixtieth minute. A couple of months after I began, in fact, I stopped advertising a one-hour rate and chose to make my minimum booking time two hours. I quickly realised that such short bookings are not only dubious in terms of time and effort versus return (travel time mattered), but it was also far too little time for me to make a connection deep enough for meaningful lovemaking. In many situations, giving the clients even just a few minutes off the clock had a big impact. Sometimes, that involved a little extra cuddling in bed, or perhaps even just a last drink together somewhere to soften the transactional truth of what we had just done. After that it was just a matter of a hug, a friendly, 'I better get out of here now' and a heartfelt, 'thank you so much'.

And Mitch was gone. As he was paid to be.

Back in the car, I was on my way to being Dan again – a dad, a son, a brother, a husband. I was also beginning to think more practically and made a mental note not to drive my heavily-branded photography van to a booking again, and that perhaps my wife's little Hyundai would be far less obtrusive. On the way home, she texted me to check how things had gone, but I wasn't ready to leave the Mitch zone right away so I messaged back to tell her my ETA and that I'd tell her all about it. I wasn't sure how I'd feel when I walked back through our front door with the scent of another woman all over me, and I felt like I needed a little 'me' time to process what I'd just done. I'd just been paid to please a woman – and it felt amazing.

When I did finally arrive home, my wife, who had obviously stayed up for me and was still in her flannel pyjamas, greeted me at the door. I waved the cash at her with a cheeky grin and reached for her. It felt like we'd both accomplished something that night and my love for her seemed to intensify. We were both happy. We'd made a great team and neither of us felt any remorse whatsoever. In fact, I thought I might even have noticed a hint of pride as my wife skipped around, wanting to know everything. I didn't want to be the kiss-and-tell type, though, so I told her a little bit about how things played out but left enough gaps to give my client the respect she deserved as well. And so, another tightrope began to emerge...

The next day, the friend who initially contacted me kindly texted me to let me know her friend had a 'magnificent' time. She also mentioned that she had organised an upcoming hen's night and was hoping I might be interested in taking part in the festivities – as a stripper. I was definitely flattered but suggested that forcing her guests to watch a 41-year-old man awkwardly dancing around naked would probably do more harm than good.

Things felt so natural and right that I wondered why I hadn't considered escorting years before. Life seemed sweeter than it had felt in a long time. And I felt like I could do anything. It was a change in me that my wife could not have failed to notice and while it added fresh energy and strength of our union in many ways, we were also proving ourselves to be only human in many other ways. When someone in a partnership suddenly seems happier, or more motivated about their appearance and the way they are seen through the eyes of others, it's natural for the other person in that partnership to second guess themselves and wonder why they were not enough.

I never wished for my wife to feel any self-doubt, so I looked for any sign that she wasn't as happy with my decision as she claimed to be. We talked about it all the time and I honestly believed she was okay with it. Maybe it was too good to be true, but in my own eyes, the world around me had suddenly become so beautifully rose-coloured that I was positive she could see the fresh new hue as clearly as I could. I was genuinely happy and I wanted the only other person in the world who knew what I was doing to be happy with me.

Chapter 3 – Decisions

The problem with all that, though, is that I was an idiot.

I was blinded by my abilities and my fairy tale wishes for how our world could be. I didn't realise it then, but the day I decided to become a male escort was also the day I began the end of my marriage. Phenomenal lack of insight, I agree.

There was a blissful ignorance to us, as a couple, as we waded through what felt like an unchartered ocean. Or perhaps I was the only ignorant one. We weren't the first couple who'd let extra-marital sex encroach upon their union, and I guarantee we won't be the last, but that doesn't change the fact that we were both naïve about the impact it would have and how we'd navigate it.

During that time, our marriage could best be described as three-parts-reality mixed with seven-parts-adventure. When I wasn't working out or shopping for fancy new clothes, I'd be at home, often with my head down and completely absent while I messaged and emailed new and existing clients.

After six months of transactional sex becoming the extra setting at our relationship table, things began to shift.

My wife's curiosity lessened and, for me, coming back home after work was less about counting the cash and more about pouring myself a few drinks to wash away Mitch in order to become Dan again. The truth is, sex workers aren't made of Teflon, and it didn't take long for the job to leave something stuck to me with each new booking.

In the case of my new client Sam, it was the impossible gravity of life itself. What goes up really does come down and by engaging with her, the pressing weight of invisible forces was palpable, even from her friend's first email to me. The thought of someone choosing me to be their sexual companion as a response to such a devastating diagnosis felt like an immense privilege. But I knew it was also going to be a huge responsibility. I wasn't sure I had the mental fortitude to be of any use to her long term.

I clearly remember receiving an email from Sam's friend on the day I'd arranged to meet her and the thoughts that raced through my head afterward. Here's what it said:

Hi Mitch, you are meeting my amazing friend Sam Sheridan tonight. Perhaps it isn't right for me to contact you, but I feel it is necessary to let you know a few things in confidence. Sam was diagnosed in January this year with early-onset Alzheimer's disease. It's in its early stages at the moment, but will gradually eat away at Sam's brain over the next 2–5 years until she can no longer remember anyone or anything.

What makes it so hard for her is that she and her ex-husband separated early last year, and she realises it will be pointless to meet someone, so she has chosen you to be that regular person with whom she can escape all the terrible stuff. I doubt you will notice anything tonight, with the exception of simple forgetfulness, and I suspect she may have already lost many of the things that would normally prevent her from spending time with you.

All I am concerned with is that she makes it home safely. I know it's not necessarily safe to give a stranger her address, but here it is: [removed], in case she can't remember and wants to go home. We love Sam, and desperately want this to be a happy event for her so we want to help, but we also want to ensure that this is her secret thing. My phone number is [removed] and her friend's is [removed] if she needs picking up for any reason.

I don't want to scare you, and I think this will be a lovely (and hopefully regular) appointment for you with a funny, smart and loyal woman who always knows what she wants, and makes it happen. Sam doesn't know I am contacting you, and I would really appreciate it if you kept it that way.

Have fun tonight.

Every industry has its own lexicon, and one that I learned very early on when I looked into the sex work world was this one: 'provider'.

At first glance, it might seem old-school and anti-feminist, as if I am some 'Great Male Provider' of the basics a woman yearns for. But it's a word that female sex workers use to describe themselves, too. Being a provider is about offering a service someone needs or wants and in today's sex industry; it's one of the preferred terms, along with 'companion', that has seen 'prostitute' now rightfully considered as offensive as it sounds.

Sam choosing me as someone to help her hold onto an important part of her life as a woman was a real test of whether I could actually do what my directory listing said I could. Was I genuinely a 'provider'? I'd been in the business for six months, and all of my appointments had been either one-off interactions or had been the occasional repeat booking with women who'd obviously enjoyed a previous experience. Ongoing companionship bookings had not been part of it and now, here it was, in the form of a high-achieving former CEO and mother of two young children, asking me to take her by the hand and walk, together, into a fragile, inevitable sunset – with some wine, fine food, interesting conversation and passionate lovemaking all part of our journey.

The pre-first date communication from the friend who'd been instrumental in hiring me had set the scene by telling me that our initial three-hour booking could be a starting point for something very regular. Of course, it was all dependent on whether Sam felt that 'click' with me and, for my part, I needed to be just as sure I was happy to be part of the plan. What I knew about early-onset Alzheimer's was limited, but I did some research and realised that Sam's decline might be very rapid.

When I told my wife about my hesitations, she encouraged me and prodded me towards taking on the challenge. Her enthusiasm may have been because she was a doctor, so she tended to view things in a slightly detached, clinical way. In her eyes, Sam was a woman who needed a multi-faceted approach to her wellbeing, and if that included an additional 'specialist' to help her feel desirable and cared for, then she had every right to do what it took to access those feelings. Here was a once-vibrant woman who had an incredibly impressive career and a gorgeous young family and, because her separation had coincided with her diagnosis, she was not only facing an uncertain future – she was also facing it in a sort of isolation. While she still had the essence of her sexuality and womanhood to hold onto, she was clearly keen to explore it before the memories of this aspect of herself dimmed with the rest of her remembrances.

Asking myself if I had the strength to be part of that was something I didn't take lightly. I genuinely wanted to make the last few years of Sam's life as comfortable and stimulating as possible but, because it was difficult separating Dan from Mitch, I had to first determine whether I could have feelings for her. Essentially, I needed to know if I could love her. I realised that perhaps I was overthinking things though, and knew that the only way forward was to just live in the moment, go on that first booking, and see where it took me.

I went through the usual afternoon routine of primping and preening, in the same way I believed all my clients deserved.

I showered, trimmed, shaved and plucked myself before throwing on one of my nice suits and a hint of cologne. I was always nervous before work, but this time the feeling was heightened by my concerns about how Sam would present and how much of a hold her illness already had on her.

As the time drew nearer, I found myself reaching for a quick line of coke to get me through. Yes, another cliché, I know, but as the pressure of the job started to get on top of me, I sometimes found myself having a quick bump as a pick-me-up if I wasn't feeling particularly energetic or sociable. I told myself it was just a temporary fix, though – I knew I'd be fine.

The GPS directed me to an inner-suburban apartment complex and after I pulled up and gave myself one last check in the mirror, I shook a small amount onto the smooth screen of one of my phones and had a good sniff through a rolled up fifty dollar note. Not too much though – just enough to encourage confidence, without affecting my performance...

Chapter 4 – Anna

Whenever I'm serious about someone, I've always been the breed of guy who operates on a one-woman-at-a-time basis. As an escort, though, it became my job to have multiple girlfriends. There were still the one-off bookings that served as the marking of a special occasion – a birthday present from friends, a birthday present bought by the client themselves or sometimes a booking designed to say goodbye to a painful past. Increasingly, however, my working life involved repeat bookings, and this came with its own unique set of issues.

I've been around long enough to know that for many people, the separation between sex and love can be a road that's paved with hurt feelings and poor self-esteem. It was that way for me, too. Sex is obviously intimate, but as I entered my forties, it felt even more intense. Saliva, sweat and skin-on-skin closeness puts smells, sounds and all kinds of sights in your face. Literally. It's pure and so very natural but at the same time, it can be intensely complex. If I was clinical about my own approach to sex with a client, neither one of us would enjoy it. If I remained detached, then it was just a job and I was an object. To make it real as an escort, I had to look for a connection that would elevate the naked flesh I was being paid to caress, cuddle and copulate with, to the status of someone I cared enough about to want to pleasure, even if it didn't necessarily pleasure me.

Respect is a critical thing for me and that had to be genuine too. By letting respect guide everything I did, being kind came next and as an escort, my brand of kindness was sharing more than just my body. I also shared something of my soul. It was to my detriment in many ways, but if laying myself bare ever felt too raw or too damn terrifying, there was always a bit of coke around to restore the equilibrium and keep my emotions light.

Managing my mental health had always been a maze of self-medication – from alcohol, to weed, to anti-depressants – and in a way, Mitch became another drug to prop me up by opening the door to another reality. As Mitch, I could see beauty in just about anyone. Even myself. Mitch also helped me cope during those times when clients weren't always the 'type' I would usually pursue in my daily life as Dan. Mitch saw through physical imperfections by focusing on emotions: kindness, warmth, compassion. And with that approach, he had the capacity to love almost every woman.

Every now and then, however, there was a woman who was extra special – and Anna was one of them. I first spoke to her at about 10.30 pm after a booking I'd just finished in the Melbourne CBD. I'd already advertised a trip to Brisbane, where I planned to visit some regular clients while hopefully meeting some new ones, and Anna was hoping to be one.

The booking that night had gone well and I was ready for some downtime when a call came through from a woman with a sweet-sounding voice that told me she was quite lonely and wasn't entirely sure what prompted her to call me. I was sitting on some grass next to my car in a service station car park, snacking on a lukewarm pie and on the edge of that euphoria/flatness that tended to hit me at the end of each booking. Anna was, she said, all alone in her place, almost two thousand clicks north in Brisbane just looking up at the stars. So I turned my eyes skyward and listened to her.

'I'm not sure what I'm doing,' she said, 'but I'm lonely and this just feels right.'

Under the open sky, I could see the same stars and I suddenly felt all alone too. Because she was in Brisbane and I was in Melbourne, there was no rushing or urgency about it, but with my tour coming up the following week, she quickly paid her deposit so I would lock her in. In between, we exchanged more texts as well as teasing voice messages that created a kind of tightrope of sexual tension between us. And then came our night...

She'd booked me for three hours and I was as meticulous as ever with my grooming routine. I was really excited to meet her and was already hoping that she might become a regular client. I was also super nervous. I didn't have anything illicit to calm me down, so I cranked up some Radiohead and sang away to help ease the tension. After receiving the five-minute warning from her, I went downstairs and waited for her to collect me. When the limo arrived and I saw a gorgeous woman step out to greet me, I felt instant relief. She was stunning. Yes, Mitch can find something to love in all women but it's always an added happiness when somebody is just Your Type. She was wearing a flowing navy dress with thin straps and a subtly plunging neckline, no jewellery and a beautiful, warm smile. Her blonde hair hung straight past her toned shoulders and the high heels she wore accentuated her beautifully toned calves – the result of either the farm work she did or perhaps due to many hours spent in the gym. She was wearing minimal makeup, and clearly didn't need to. Given the public location, I kissed her hand and kept my distance, and suggested that perhaps we should head to the car as I did my best to look more bodyguard than escort.

We had a wonderful ride and our conversation remained light whilst in the company of our driver, but turned more personal during dinner. She told me that she could tell I was a good person because of how friendly I was to the driver. Her ex-husband, she said, would have been disparaging and dismissive, and it was my first glimpse into the marriage she'd courageously left behind. As our conversation intensified, I gained more of an insight into a man whose greed and ego would cost him a life with this amazing woman. Both Anna and her husband were successful business people, and they managed to hold onto the marriage as they built a company worth millions, but then very quickly he treated her as if she was a poorly performing employee when his true self-centred and materialistic nature emerged. Suddenly 'their money' became 'his money'. Any dreams Anna had outside of the business were quickly dismissed as a waste of money and therefore not worthy of consideration.

Despite some of these heavier conversations, or perhaps *because* of these heavier conversations, Anna and I ended up having a great night. We bonded over our love of animals, and this former country girl had lots of stories about the pigs and chickens she'd been adopting as rescue animals. It almost felt like she was a safe haven for me as well.

She was initially quite shy but our dry and sarcastic senses of humour matched perfectly, so it soon became like we were old friends. That heart-on-sleeve characteristic of mine to be real, however, meant that I found myself getting once again quite emotional and a little angry when she told me about her own childhood trauma and the bullying and belittling she'd experienced from her ex-husband and his relatives.

I learned an early lesson that night and it was one I am thankful for. At one point throughout our dinner, Anna told me that she was concerned that I was getting too emotional when she told me about how she had been treated. It was a revelation to me and it's now a constant reminder of why Mitch exists in the first place. Dan can't take other people's trauma on at every booking and Dan can't do what I would want to do in normal life, which is fix the situation and throttle her ex – or at least trash his Ferrari. I'm nothing special, I know. I'm no vigilante, but that said, a sharp jab to his cologned, well-moisturised and possibly surgically enhanced jaw did sound quite therapeutic to me. Clients didn't hire me to just vent their anger, though. Okay, well, some did – and that was fine with me, but mostly, I was there to help them escape those negative emotions. I was definitely not a solution to their relationship troubles but saw myself as just another caring human being with two ears, a caring heart and a desire to help them as best I could.

Anna asked me if I could stay the whole night and when we eventually made love, it was very slow going. We were both clearly attracted to each other, but I could sense that she was being quite guarded. I couldn't tell whether it was her body or her heart she was protecting and at one point while I was on top of her, I noticed that she was pushing against me – as if she was uncomfortable with something. To me, it felt unnatural, so I stopped and gently checked in with her to see if she was okay. I'd already experienced bookings with clients who had trusted me with their heartbreaking stories of abuse, so the warning signs were there and I was always hyper-alert to any discomfort. Their grief was palpable and although it surprised me at first that any woman with violence in her past would feel comfortable enough to seek out a sexual interaction with a stranger, it made sense to me soon after. They saw me as safe and predictable. I wasn't a Tinder date that could portray himself one way and then turn out to be something different and terrifying. I was a service provider who could be tracked and traced and even came with testimonials from other happy clients:

'Mitch is very attentive. I felt completely safe at all times. His generosity meant that he tailored the booking specifically to incorporate an activity that I love.'

'Life is meant to be enjoyed and with Mitch by your side, it will be a wonderful gift to yourself!'

'I have just had an amazing night with Mitch. He is a real gentleman, sexy, an excellent kisser, and has a beautiful soul.'

Anna knew exactly what I meant when I asked her and although her actions weren't related to violence, they were related to control. She told me that she deliberately did that because her husband said she 'didn't fuck hard enough' and that she hated it. I struggled to keep my thoughts to myself and instead kissed and stroked her soft skin while telling her that this was all about her this time. I encouraged her to focus on what made *her* feel better and I hoped she felt comfortable enough to show me exactly what she liked.

When I left in the morning, the smile on my face was as real as it got and I wondered, for the first time since starting this work, what might happen if I fell too hard for a client.

And so, my heart became even more confused...

Chapter 5 — Mitch's Flop-Tastic Foray

I once met a couple in South Yarra who used male escorts as playthings.

Quite literally.

They would scroll through the various directories and order us like pizzas.

This was early on in my career and I should've known better, but five hours was a huge booking for me back then. When I arrived, I immediately noticed the money they had. As the doors to their private elevator opened to the huge reception area, I was greeted by a gorgeously crazy woman with lusciously long and curly dark hair wearing nothing but a big, beautiful smile and an English football jersey. It was Manchester United from memory. After a very warm and wonderful greeting, I met her husband and another incredibly beautiful woman who, I was told, often joined in on their fun. The husband seemed friendly, but his stern gaze and ultra-firm handshake reminded me that I was the hired help and that he was the alpha male of the house. Straight away though, I was told, anything went that night.

And it did.

There were endless lines of coke, several bags of what looked like MDMA and quite the array of sex toys – sterilised and nicely arranged.

I'd still only been doing the job for a few months at that stage and had become accustomed to random enquires from all sorts of people – including couples. I eventually chose not to offer my services to couples but in those early days, I was still finding my feet, which had been quite dramatically swept away in the initial excitement of exploring this strange new sexual world. Testing one's limits is tricky at the best of times. Back then, it felt even more challenging and seemed to vacillate between feelings where I was on top of the world and in control and other moments, which seemed to be increasing, when I didn't have a clue what was going on and how to deal with it. And that was one of those times.

The three of them had obviously been partying for hours. Perhaps days. They were funny, friendly and completely wasted. I arrived sober but that changed pretty quickly. There was lots of nudity, a huge spa and many, many visits to that drug-filled tabletop. But the thing about drugs and sex is that although all inhibitions go out the window, the ability to act on them rapidly descends into a sort of soft-on cuddle-fest, where orgasms are impossible but physical contact and kissing can be just as nice.

And that is basically how that night (and most of the morning) transpired. Most of the time, however, my guard was as flaccid as the rest of me and once the fog cleared a couple of days later, I vowed never to get myself in that kind of situation again. As a male escort, I needed to be in control, and my role was to guide my client through to their desired outcome in a way that was safe and sexy. That night, I was roaming around that fancy apartment like a lost puppy and I was definitely not in control.

When I got an invitation to be in an adult film a few weeks

later though, that control felt like it was coming back, and I saw it as an opportunity to launch my Mitch persona on a whole new audience. I've always tried to take every opportunity as it comes in life and after all, I'd already had that pseudo-orgy with three people I'd never previously met, so how different would it be to have a camera there? The woman who ran the production company reached out to me on Twitter. There was no audition – just a paid flight to Sydney, an agreed sum for the performance and a surprisingly long script to explain the ridiculous 'plot' which, in a nutshell, required me to play the role of a busy businessman who just happened to run into an old flame in a massage parlour.

And there I was. In a beautiful apartment overlooking Bondi Beach with a female co-star who was almost too stunning to be real and my wacky dream that this was somehow a big break. By way of research, I'd watched a lot of porn, including scenes featuring my co-star and I saw it with a photographer's eye, taking note of camera angles and how I'd be expected to move to give the best possible impact on screen. Still, I was absolutely terrified. There was a mound of paperwork to sign, including the results of a medical examination I needed to show to prove I was clean and clear. Then, for extra safety, there was an on-set visual examination to ensure there were no other obvious conditions.

We got the initial dialogue out of the way and then various sexual positions were discussed and agreed upon. It was all very professional and clinical, which just added to my angst. I was told that once the camera captured enough, the director would give me a five-minute countdown to come on my co-star's stomach, chest, arse or wherever gave the best view. And that's when I got completely camera-shy. As I came to the realisation that I would need to become erect and ejaculate on cue, my body let me down. I'll forever be thankful to my co-star for her professionalism after she reassured me that I was far from the first to suffer this problem, before proceeding to enthusiastically suck on my overcooked cannelloni in order to get some sort of footage... but I was a lost cause. Stating the obvious, the producer piled on more pressure by telling me to leave the room and to just 'come out hard'. As a policy and for my co-star's safety, I wasn't allowed any time alone with her, which definitely would have helped given my need to know who I'm fucking in order to find some kind of emotional connection, so I was well and truly doomed.

I tried to remain calm and took myself out to the next room to watch porn on my phone in an attempt to get myself back in the mood. But I couldn't get it up, no matter how much I tried. I just couldn't get the image of everyone out there waiting for me. I even went for a walk and called my wife who, bless her, sent me a risqué photo I'd taken of her in an attempt to get me turned on. But no dice.

It was a complete head-fuck. They stopped production for the day and after a virtually sleepless night, I returned the next morning in an even worse state than before. The woman who'd invited me asked for the production money back, booked me on a flight back home to Melbourne and I was sent home with my tail (and my flaccid cock) between my legs.

I'd failed.

I never saw the end result, but I think the producer's vision for this cinematic tour de force transitioned into a girl-on-girl scene with another actress in lieu of me. An attempt was made to massage my fragile ego by telling me the acting side of my performance was great. It was just a pity about the erection.

Do I want to be in another porn film? Absolutely not.

My vision of dominating the adult film industry had been born and killed within just a few months of wending my way into the sex industry and in hindsight, because I never actually wanted to be a porn star at all, I admit that I'm glad. Funnily enough though, my high school principal once told me that he thought I should be an actor (I was a bit of a smartass) but somehow, I don't think that's what he had in mind.

Chapter 6 – Meeting Sam

It was finally time.

As 7 pm approached, I licked any remaining coke from the screen of my phone, hopped out of the car and walked the short distance to her apartment building. It was a wet and miserable night but I barely noticed. I was actually more excited than nervous on that occasion given the possibility she could become one of my regular clients – and 'regs' are your bread and butter in the sex work world. I buzzed the apartment number I'd been given and heard a disembodied voice through the intercom. She was coming down to greet me. It was that busy time of night when people were heading out or coming home after a long day and I may have looked too closely at a few different women weaving their way through the foyer before I noticed a woman with short black hair making her way towards me. She'd specified a three-hour 'boyfriend experience' with the option to extend if necessary. The format of a 'boyfriend experience' booking is to treat the booking like a typical date where you go out to dinner or stay in and maybe watch a movie. This can be distinguished from what is known as a 'porn star experience' which is... I have no idea, to be honest. At least when it comes to male escorting anyway. Maybe there's someone else there stressing you out to get hard on command, or something.

Because we were heading out, Sam was already dressed in a bulky jacket and it took her several more steps along the long corridor before she was close enough for me to make her out clearly. Her lack of shyness, combined with her friendly features and beautiful, warm smile was immediately disarming. I wasn't sure if it was her high-flying corporate history or the Alzheimer's already taking the edge off a strange situation that made her come across as completely relaxed and chilled out – but it certainly helped me feel comfortable. As I mentioned, I can't initiate anything in public with clients, due to the discretion that goes hand-in-hand with what I do so, after a friendly, business-like greeting, we focused on where to eat.

The high-priced tapas bar across the road seemed like an easy choice but because neither of us was drinking alcohol that night, the social crutch of a cocktail or two was missing and it was an effort to fill the gaps in what was already becoming a growing number of awkward silences. When she mentioned that she was no longer able to drive, it was the first time she alluded to her condition and I simply nodded, wondering if she'd tell me more. She didn't, so I quickly moved the conversation to more comfortable topics.

After about an hour, I asked Sam if she wanted to show me her apartment. I wasn't sure if she was aware that her friend had emailed me and, because she hadn't specifically mentioned anything, it felt like we were dancing around the edge of a crater that neither of us wanted to fall into. And then, as we got up to leave, she just said it – very matter-of-factly:

'I've been diagnosed with early-onset Alzheimer's and I might forget a few things. I just wanted to let you know.'

It was as though she'd been trying to tell me all night and when she finally did, there was no hint of concern, self-judgement or embarrassment. I already liked her a lot. If I hadn't already known, the truth was that I probably would've assumed she was a bit of a daydreamer – and assumed she wasn't driving for legal reasons. I tried to be upbeat but still concerned, and said something like, 'Oh, I'm really sorry to hear that – we don't have to talk about that unless you want to.' I didn't want to dismiss her declaration, but she was paying me for the experience of a male escort and I just wanted to keep it light and fun to start with.

Dan was already getting in the way of Mitch's moves, however, and I distinctly remember cuddling her, stroking her hair, looking into her eyes and feeling my heart ache for everything she was about to lose. This woman with the lovely voice and beautiful persona was already slipping away into a kind of void from which she couldn't escape, but now I had to stop thinking about that and turn the evening into a sexy romp. It was really tough not to falter. That sharp intelligence I'd been told she possessed was still visible, but it felt softened by her obvious vulnerability.

She hadn't seen an escort before and I guided her through the first steps by asking permission to hug and kiss her, giving her ownership of every decision and doing my best to make her feel at ease. We set up a speaker, had the usual debate about whether eighties or nineties music was better, and when I led her into the bedroom, I saw her in a way I imagined she might have seen herself in an old photo album. She was a woman who was very much connected to her young body, even if the link with her mind was changing. She knew when she wanted to be in control and when she felt comfortable enough to let me take the lead, and it all concluded in an embrace that was gentle, sweet and filled with love and understanding.

We said goodbye after talking about meeting again. The 'click' had happened for her, which was a flattering boost to my self-esteem, and although I knew I would honour that commitment and see her again – and again, for as long as she wanted to – part of me was already feeling too emotionally invested, and wondering whether I could be a companion to both a wonderful woman *and* a debilitating disease.

Chapter 7 –
The Trials of Adolescence

When you're young, you don't recognise your own depression. You don't know the word and, even if you do, you don't associate it with mood swings, worries, paranoia or other negative thoughts that begin to worm their way into at least one part of every single day.

I always had a fascination with darker things, like murder and crime, and the scarier side of life. When I was in grade six, there were some seedy guys in a gang from my neighbourhood who put the word out that they wanted to 'bash' me. I was so convinced that serious harm was going to come to me that I wrote a little letter and hid it behind a poster on my bedroom wall for my parents to find in the event of my inevitable demise.

If anything ever happens to me and I get murdered, ask around for ___ because they will be the ones that did it.

That was a rough year for me. A few months after my bullying scare, I was enjoying the peace of a beautiful morning, pedalling my way through my regular paper delivery route, when a rather chubby, sweaty middle-aged man in running shorts and a undersized singlet lumbered up to me and commented on my bike, which I was, incidentally, quite proud of. When you're young and you've been raised to be well-mannered, your first instinct is to be polite, so I think I muttered back a quick 'thanks' and continued doing what I was being paid to do. Looking back now, as a world-weary man, it's obvious what this predator wanted, but at the time I just thought it strange (and then, quite scary) when he then asked me for a 'dink'.

As kids, we'd all given rides to people, but having this grown man climb onto the back of my little bike to hug me felt more than terrifying. He was somehow straddled on the cargo rack, which also made it difficult to reach my newspapers. My vision seemed to go monochrome and my mind just went blank, so I just kept trying to deliver my papers with this concerning new passenger weighing me down. I guess it was a kind of denial that made me try to carry on with my usual work routine, but as I struggled to peddle with him on the back, he undid my reflective vest and put his hand on my crotch.

And that was too much for me.

My anger gave me immediate clarity and the resolve to get rid of that weird guy. I'm so grateful to the fiercely independent little boy I was because, if I hadn't found the courage to save myself by forcing him off the bike by basically dropping it and firmly asking him to leave me alone, I'm not sure what might have happened. My thoughts in childhood were often cloudy and creepy, and because I thought I'd somehow done something wrong, it took me ages to tell my dad. It no doubt shocked the hell out of him because from that day onwards he followed me in his car, to keep me safe.

My dad is a very intelligent man and someone I have much respect for. He's an academic, whilst my mother worked in healthcare. We were a kind of middle-class/working-class family that seemed as familiar as every family around us, but the difference I could already see was that the Old Man was often troubled or distracted. It took him a while to be officially diagnosed as depressed, but when he finally was, and despite his initial trepidation and the stigma that came with it, he took medication and his heavy burdens seemed to lift. He'd come from parents who had their own issues, with my grandfather, in particular, finding happiness elusive. Out of respect, though, those stories aren't mine to tell.

Then there's Mum – from good Baltic stock and an incredibly loving and caring human being. If she was the perfect mother in my eyes, she's become an even more perfect grandmother to my son. We share similarities, too. My mother seems to be constantly worried and, in those rare moments that she's not worried, she's worried about not being worried. Despite this, I feel as though we also share the quality of being fairly laid-back, and unconcerned about minor details. Deep down, we know everything will be okay in the end. Her strong resolve may have stemmed from the fact that she's been battling rheumatoid arthritis for most of her adult life. I still remember her quietly sobbing in her bedroom when I was a kid, due to the pain she constantly experienced and how proud I was of myself when she taught me how to wrap her bandages. The courage she showed back then, and the kindness she showed her patients as a nurse, are two reasons why I admire healthcare workers so much to this day.

Chapter 8 – Pussies Galore

When business was slow, I'd usually find myself eagerly looking at my phone in the morning, in the hopes that I'd received an enquiry from the night before, and if that happened, more often than not, I'd blindly accept any opportunity that presented itself. This was good for the finances, but it often put me in awkward positions.

With this particular client, the basics seemed okay for starters. She described herself as a petite brunette with 'girl next door good looks', and, as the image of her face flashed up on my phone in the photo she'd sent me, I saw a woman who appeared to be in her mid-thirties, with a friendly smile, lovely and thick blonde hair and soft brown eyes. To me, it was a no-brainer – especially as she wanted me there overnight, which meant very good money. We ended up chatting a couple of times on the phone to get the flirtatious vibe going, and even though she came across as kind of dorky, I thought that to be fairly endearing. When it was time to finally meet, I was my usual ball of anxiety, mingled with a tinge of excitement that I was going to be touching and tasting another person who I already knew to be quite beautiful. My internal conflict seemed to eat me alive at times.

I'd stuck to my routine and preparation rituals. I ensured that I was neat and tidy downstairs and a gym session that morning had left me feeling strong and powerful. I was freshly showered and cologned, and even though my teeth had been flossed and brushed to a shiny freshness, I still grabbed the breath mints I always sucked on for the drive there. For me, first impressions were everything. When a woman booked my time – especially for an overnighter – it was a huge investment of both money and trust, and I wanted things to go perfectly from the start.

The drive was a long one, made worse by the traffic and lack of parking, so I messaged to tell her I'd be a little late. As I walked towards her front door, my hands smoothed the jacket I'd put on over a crisp white shirt before I reached up to knock.

When she opened the door, it was the smell that hit me first.

She answered with that beautiful smile and, as I leaned in to peck her cheek, my nostrils took in the full scent. It was the pungent smell of lots of animals. Cats, to be precise. And it smelled like their cat litter had not been changed for a very long time.

'Come in, babe – just put your bag anywhere,' she said as she took my hand to lead me along her carpeted hallway. It was dimly lit, and it would've added some kind of ambience but for the stench of fresh cat shit and very old cat piss that attacked my nasal cavities with a vengeance. I was wearing some particularly nice Bally loafers and my feet seemed to automatically lift higher, as if scared to land in something undetected. In the living room, by the light of a lamp in the corner of the room, I could see something furry moving on the couch and she swept her hand along the cushions to push a cute little kitten to one side before offering me a seat. She must've noticed my concern.

'Oh no! You're not allergic, are you?' she asked.

'Ah – no, no, not at all,' I said, trying to sound as chilled as possible. I tried to recover and didn't want to stay quiet for too long. 'I love animals too.'

'I know!' she said, all excited. 'I saw that on Twitter!'

I tried to initiate some small talk to help both of us relax, but with cats of various shapes and sizes continuing to move through the living room, as if it was the setting for a David Attenborough documentary, I struggled to stay focused and was immediately concerned about getting that all-important erection. In all honesty, I'm probably only talking about five or six cats, but given how intimate her little house was, space was very limited and I was damned if my naked body was going anywhere near those things.

She told me she was single and had been for quite a while and she wanted me there that night to just feel the warmth of a man next to her as she slept. She loved her 'fur-babies', but she really missed the feeling of a man's whole-body embrace as she slept. Her honesty was refreshing and sweet but, in combination with the cat obsession, the impact on me wasn't the greatest aphrodisiac. I asked to use her bathroom, and it was there that I noticed the first of many trays filled with clumps of soggy blobs and god-awful strips of brown cat shit – sitting right next to the toilet itself.

On my way back to the living room, I headed through the kitchen, where another stinky litter tray had its home next to the rubbish bin. It wasn't all bad, though – those initial faecal discoveries proved very useful when I attempted to navigate my way through her house later that night.

To be fair, her house was clean in every other way – it was uncluttered, nicely decorated and spacious enough, but when a cat leapt down from the dining table after drinking from a glass of water that had been left there, I made a mental note to keep anything I ate or drank from within eyeshot at all times. I was there for a reason though and, as I stepped back into the living room, I practiced a bit of mindful breathing to calm myself enough to be convinced that I wouldn't panic and that I would make it work – somehow. This lovely lady was paying me a lot of money to feel special and I knew I couldn't let her down.

We talked some more and I suggested we throw on some music and cuddle for a while. I then asked if she'd like me to kiss her and she nodded emphatically. She was a rigid but gentle kisser and as I held her, I felt the outlines of another beautiful body.

Okay, I thought, *now we're getting somewhere...* At least *she* smelled beautiful. I immediately started to feel a lot better – made evident by the increasing bulge in my pants.

'Can we go to my bedroom?' she asked.

She took my hand to lead me into a nearby room. As my eyes adjusted to the dim candlelight, I saw more movement and another furry little body and, oh man, another bloody cat! She laughed as she pushed the fluffball to one side in an attempt to put her head on her pillow.

'Jazzy doesn't like sharing her bed,' she said.

And it seemed that Jazzy really didn't.

The cat looked perpetually grumpy with a broad flat nose and a bad attitude. I immediately didn't like it and I could tell the feeling was mutual. I offered to undress my client, but asked if she could move the grumpy black-and-white beast off the pillow first. I was damned if I was going to have sex with that next to me. I'm the same with any pet for that matter; I don't know why people think it's okay. There's a time and place for animals, and when there's nudity involved, I draw the line. Irritatingly, she declined my request.

'She gets grumpy when she gets woken up,' I was told.

This one was non-negotiable, so I took it upon myself to respectfully, but firmly, get rid of the stupid thing by hooking my hand under it before flicking it off the bed. The cat didn't want to surrender its comfortable, warm position but after a couple of attempts, I had it on the floor.

The workbench now clear and with my client sitting on the edge of the bed, I was able to kneel in front of her and let my hands slowly move up her body to tease her under her t-shirt. After a while, I pushed her back on the bed and took off her jeans. Her skin was soft, warm and youthful and I found myself falling into that natural state of arousal that comes from the sensory pleasure of skin-on-skin contact. She helped me take my shirt off before I took the rest of my clothes off – hard as a rock now and super excited.

She was already moaning softly and as I let my lips follow the trace of my fingers against her lacy, cream-coloured underwear, I gently massaged her clit and felt her tremble. I played with her for a little longer to tease her and the moisture of my mouth and her own wetness made her underwear tight against her skin. The memory of the cat still lingered but at that point, with my nose and mouth between her legs, I'd found another world to escape to and I was in the moment. Pure Mitch – completely focused on giving my wonderful client pleasure as my tongue and fingers explored her. She arched her back and pushed down on the back of my head. I could tell by her constant, rhythmic movements that she was close to coming.

'OW!'

That fucking cat scratched me!

'Jazzy, darling, what's wrong?' she calmly asked the damn thing.

My client seemed more worried about my new arch enemy than me and I had to excuse myself to stumble off to the bathroom to look in the mirror, only to see a red welt already showing on my arse cheek. I used some warm water and hand soap from the basin in an attempt to wash away the germs I was concerned were already creeping into my bloodstream.

'You okay, babe?' she called from the bedroom.

It'd only been a few minutes but I could hear a little hint of irritation in her voice. I had left her half-naked on the bed on the verge of an orgasm, after all.

'Yep – absolutely,' I replied as I walked back in. 'Now, where were we?'

Cat Lady was still on the bed, patting Jazzy the Attacker, who was lying right next to her naked groin. I immediately thought of the cat shit everywhere and of all those microscopic hairs getting in my mouth and it just grossed me out. Meanwhile, my client was motioning with her other hand to get me to come back to that place between her legs.

'I was really getting into that.' She smiled. 'You really know what you're doing, don't you?'

She annoyingly put the cat back on the bed near the pillows and it looked like it was staying there, so I positioned myself at the foot of the bed so I was well and truly in a safe zone. As I leant forward to nibble the inside of her thigh, my eyes flicked to my watch. I'd been there ninety minutes and there was the whole night to go.

I was already dreading the lack of sleep I'd get, but, as I listened to the scrape of cat paws on the couch in the loungeroom, I wrapped myself around my client and found myself getting hard again. It was a huge relief. Jazzy was still in the vicinity, but we managed to have the first of many rounds of lovemaking.

Things flowed a bit more smoothly from then on, except for one awkward moment during the night when, after some wonderfully fast and passionate sex, I accidentally flicked the condom straight into a water bowl that was lying on the floor, past the foot of the bed. I had no idea I'd done it until my client got up to go to the toilet and freaked out about what she saw. I thought it was pretty funny, but my client was seriously pissed off. I pretended that I was just as horrified as she was and told her I would quickly head to the kitchen to thoroughly wash it out. As I stood there naked, though, I thought fondly of Jazzy and smiled to myself while I carelessly plucked the cum-filled condom out of the little bowl, left all the same water in it, and put it straight back to where it was.

Chapter 9 — Evolving

You know that character in Seinfeld who talks about himself in the third person?

Creating another persona for myself felt a little like that at times. I knew Mitch needed to maintain his marketing 'brand' – that of a carefree, successful escort at the top of his game – but this was in obvious conflict with Dan needing jobs simply to survive. Managing Mitch was an endless upkeep of everything from manscaping to manicures. I took the job of how to present Mitch to the world very seriously. I didn't see my commitment to my physical appearance as narcissistic – it was more that it was a critical component of my job, but at times it became quite exhausting. If you ended up booking Mitch, you would find a man who was meticulous about grooming and had a wardrobe that was classic and cool. But other things were brewing beneath the visage.

Mitch went to the gym and worried about his stubbornly hidden abs.

Dan drank alone most nights and weighed up the pros and cons of feeling things deeply, compared to not wanting to feel anything at all.

Mitch asked himself where the next booking was coming from,

but Dan had deeper things to be concerned about like, *how long can I do this?* Or, *how do I keep managing to pull this off?*

I often wondered if I got bored or tired of being paid to have sex with women for a living, what on Earth was there out there that could possibly hold my attention? In my upbeat moments, I believed it was quite literally the best, most perfect job for a man to have. In the darker times, though, I worried for my future, worried what my son would think of me, and worried about how my wife was coping – I worried about everything.

The balance between looking after my body and my need to manage my mental health with alcohol and drugs was a weird juggle but one I thought I'd managed well. I knew I was probably kidding myself by justifying my lifestyle, but I believed I still knew when enough was enough.

My bigger problem was that whilst my working life was all about immersion in hyper-intimacy, I found myself craving it more than ever in my private life. When I spoke to some of my female friends in the industry, it felt like they were much better at separating their work and personal lives than I was. They were just as compassionate and emotionally present when they were with their clients, but seemed to be much better at switching off afterwards. I just couldn't seem to do it, no matter how good my intentions were. My vision of a lifestyle as a sex worker never included the mental strains I felt, but it stood to reason that there would be a few surprises after such a drastic career change – and especially one I'd entered with absolutely no prior training or advice.

Don't get me wrong – for the majority of the time, the job was great. It was bloody awesome, in fact. When I was one half of a beautiful, heavenly sexual union – one that felt raw and alive and real – the endorphins would shoot through my veins like electricity, all energy and fire and timeless bliss. As the bookings continued, though, I found myself analysing each one and chastising myself for anything that didn't go to plan. If I didn't hear from a client again, I wondered, why not? Had I done something wrong? But then just as quickly, I'd realise that an experience with Mitch did not come cheaply, and so of course the majority of my clients would be one-offs. It just made financial sense. It was also interesting to note how my thinking had shifted during that time, from a focus on the money to a point where I often didn't even count it or look at it for days. It would just sit in my kitchen drawer, in nice envelopes, sometimes with beautiful little cards, only to be opened days later when I put it in the bank. Perhaps that was a good thing, though – the job was beginning to be more customer-focused and now appealed to me on a more professional level. Whenever I became concerned about my longevity and how incredibly insecure the work could be, it was reassuring to know that my goals and ethics were perhaps evolving into something greater.

On the days when my arms were wrapped around an interesting, wonderful woman, whose body had responded to my touch with a pleasure that reminded me of my value, I'd go home imagining the rest of my life being like that. I felt so buoyed by the part I'd played in making someone else feel good about themselves that it blocked out every other negative thing I'd ever felt or thought about myself. In those moments, I became a silent champion of sex work and an advocate for how it could transform your life. It was an almost missionary-like zeal. I wanted to convert and inspire and, if I'd come directly from a particularly amazing booking, I'd find myself standing in the schoolyard at pick up the next day, dying to tell the other dads just how good their lives could be if they banished any nonsense about stigma and simply embraced their wildest dreams.

But I knew better.

Chapter 10 – The Veteran

Some women choose to hire escorts instead of navigating the dating scene and many of them are quite happy to invest decent sums of money for the right companion. From my perspective, being booked by a client with that much experience with escorts could be challenging.

First, there was their attitude.

When most clients hired me, the transaction came with a healthy dose of nervousness, which created a particular dynamic. Despite *my* anxiety, the power-play was that, sure, I might not have known everything I was doing, but they knew less and, because of that, it was me who stepped into the role as guide. But when I was hired by women who had spent years paying male escorts, they came to the booking knowing exactly what they wanted from me and there were rarely any feelings of embarrassment or discomfort for me to massage away. At its worst, that level of client confidence could include a very definite vibe that they were the buyer and I was the goods.

I'd come to appreciate that I didn't like that feeling much. And when the pressure felt too great and I was aware that I was standing on the shoulders of the male escorts who'd come before me, the spectre of achieving a less than favourable comparison would fill me with so much stomach-churning dread that my inability to perform properly sometimes became a self-fulfilling prophecy.

So, there I was – in a room in one of the more dated hotels in Melbourne and painfully aware of my client's experience with multiple escorts, thanks mainly to her detailed explanation of exactly how many she had seen before me, as well as all the rich details of what was good – and sometimes very bad – about each and every one of them.

She was a reasonably attractive and fit woman in her late forties, with curly blonde hair and kind blue eyes, but she had what I would describe as more of a grimace than a smile. She looked kind of... hungry. It was obvious that she meant business when her gaze drifted immediately to my crotch within seconds of our meeting and she reached to grab my bulge in the doorway. Rushed, passionate love is fine sometimes but not when you barely know the person. She started unbuttoning my pants and, seeing how it was playing out, I asked for her to slow down so we could take our time. I didn't want things to get off to a bad start but I also didn't want to feel like a piece of meat.

Kissing, to me, is almost as intimate as sex – in fact, it's often more intimate – and, despite this particular client's experiences with men, I still felt it necessary to call a 'time out' at one point to gently request a little less tongue. After a little while, though, and once we'd settled into a better rhythm, a kind of connection finally started to form. Luckily for me, it was enough for my cock to respond – slowly but sufficiently. I quickly slipped a condom on, just in case the moment disappeared and, by focusing on her beautiful characteristics, rather than dwell on the lack of mood that had been created, we started to make love. And that was when a male escort's second-worst penis-related nightmare came true: I orgasmed.

It had been a grand total of thirty minutes and it was my job to keep her pleasured for another two and half hours, so I tried not to panic while we chatted, still naked, about our respective lives.

I discovered that she was married and ran a small but successful little business in the country, cleaning local hotels and motels. Her husband acknowledged her strong need for intimacy but was unable to satisfy her because of erectile issues. He just wanted her to be happy, so he consented to her seeing paid lovers. I've seen quite a few couples in similar situations since then and I take my hat off to them. I think it's a real testament to the strength of their relationships that they can acknowledge the basic need we have for sexual release as human beings, without letting jealousy become an issue. In almost every situation, it comes with the understanding that the provider involved is there in a purely physical sense and that any sort of emotional attachment is best avoided. This was particularly pertinent with the client I was seeing that day because a few months prior, she'd fallen deeply in love with an escort and he broke her heart by ghosting her after several bookings. My client explained to me that she had no idea what she'd done wrong and was left devastated by the uncertainty. We were both still naked under the doona at this point and when she told me, she buried her head into my chest and unexpectedly burst into tears. So, what had initially started out as a booking that felt entirely superficial, ended up becoming a pseudo-counselling session where I did whatever I could to help mend a heart broken by another male escort.

We shared a lot that afternoon.

I told her all about my worsening marital issues and she did the same. I asked her all about what it felt like to fall in love with a provider and everything she said made perfect sense. To me, it sounded as though he may have been just as intimidated by her hungry eyes and hands as I was, and that he just couldn't bring himself to tell her he wasn't comfortable seeing her anymore. I told her I thought it was a bit rough to ghost someone and that I could definitely understand why she felt the way she did.

After about forty-five minutes of intense conversation, I finally got my mojo back. I felt like I'd learned some lessons that day, not only about what my own body was capable of, but also about how clients will almost always present their strongest, most confident side to me – but I suppose that's just human nature. I just want them to know that sex workers are far more than bodies to be played with. They can help you with other aspects of your life, too – and particularly when matters of the heart are involved.

We were both happy when I became hard again and the sex was far more natural and caring the second time around – all through communication. She sunk back on the bed with a satisfied smile before she told me she felt comfortable with me and wanted to see me again. It was in that moment – and all the ones like it – that I felt genuinely suited to the job. The feeling would pass with time though, I knew. It always did. But in that moment, as I collected my payment, reached for my keys and said my goodbyes, I revelled in the reality that I had created physical and emotional pleasure for someone else, and the feeling it gave me was like a drug that softened the sharp edges of my insecurities and made me feel like I could still matter.

Chapter 11 – Some Hard Truths

I knew it was going to happen.

Separating physical pleasure from emotional connection is difficult at the best of times but in this circumstance, with the truth of Sam's future laid out before me, it was becoming even more challenging than ever.

Because I'd wanted a better understanding of what was happening to her, I'd done some Googling and what I discovered was confronting. I read about the early symptoms such as forgetting words, forgetting where you'd left things and sometimes forgetting people's names – which was concerning enough – but it was the late-stage symptoms that really scared me and probably petrified Sam. It was hopefully a few years off, but in the end, she would find it difficult to perform even the most basic bodily functions such as swallowing and walking. I read that in some cases, the patients just sit there and cry out – trapped in an incurable nightmare. I thought, *what is this utterly evil disease?*

It was important that I focused on the present, though. I had decided to be there for her and, to the best of my ability, I would be. We were at a very early stage and I felt like her confidence in me had grown. With that trust and the reduction of a filter to her thoughts and words, she'd shared so many of her feelings with me – all usually delivered with a detached acceptance of her fate. It was something that always disarmed me, no matter how many times it happened. She told me about her changing family circumstances and the ever-increasing gap between the woman she was now and her former identity as an involved, nurturing mother and supportive wife.

Her two children weren't even in high school but they seemed to be living almost exclusively with her ex-husband and his new live-in girlfriend now, and Sam seemed wearily resigned to it. It was as if she'd already reconciled her absence from their lives and decided it was better that they be weaned off her while she still had a glimmer of her past vibrancy. Before she became unrecognisable to them, and they became unrecognisable to her. I felt the same way about my relationship with my wife and son.

My nights were becoming busier and busier and, although we still lived under the same roof, I was beginning to feel like a stranger to them. She had given up asking me where I was or when I'd be home and instead found it easier to assume she just couldn't rely on me as a father anymore. She told me she'd rather make plans without me as she knew that, more often than not, I'd flake out at the last minute. It wasn't fair on her and it certainly wasn't fair on my son.

Sam and I often discussed our dissolving marriages. It seemed to bring us closer together, like we were both on the same journey. So much so, that on one particularly miserable, cold Melbourne night, we had a brief conversation I'll never forget. It felt like a turning point in our relationship – a significant moment whereby our bond seemed to strengthen with just a few innocent words. We were cuddling under her blanket, listening to some Rüfüs Du Sol when, as I was stroking her hair, she asked me who the most important person in my life was. My answer came easily.

'My son.'

I asked her the same question and thought I knew what her

answer would be, but as she opened her mouth and looked into my eyes, that ache in my heart burrowed in even deeper.

'You are.'

I thought it might've been the disease talking, but it wasn't said with any confusion, hesitation or even emotion – it was simply a fact to her.

'What about your kids?' I asked.

She abruptly untangled herself and rolled away from me. 'They don't need me any more.'

Her response didn't surprise me, given how redundant her husband had begun to make her feel. The sad truth was that her kids did need to learn to adapt to life without her and being a parent myself, the thought of not seeing my boy turn into a man crushed me inside.

Chapter 12 – The Mental Health and Drug Chapter

My diagnosis came in my early twenties. I'd been cutting myself in the bleaker moments as an adolescent – enjoying the 'challenge' of withstanding the pain and enjoying the feeling of control. My skin still holds the memories of those times, in the faint, raised lines that criss-cross my flesh in places I thought nobody would notice. I used to see them in my reflection in the mirror as I stepped in or out of the shower and the response usually went one of two ways: sometimes, I felt stupid and reached for some cream or a few band-aids in a vague attempt to help the healing process but at other times, when in the pits of deep shame, I would sometimes reach for the blade again to create the beginnings of a new scar, as a way of punishing myself for what had already been damaged.

On the flip-side, in the creative bursts of energy that would regularly hit me like a tidal wave, I would write endlessly or pull out my camera and lighting equipment. When I was much younger, while some teenage boys might've spent hours crafting tales of science fiction and adventure, I used to write short porno stories on a clunky old green-and-black-screened IBM computer. That early interest in the female form is something I'd have to partially credit my uncle for, I think. My version of a 'birds and bees' talk had been as good as non-existent, but I'd always been attracted to 'naughty things' and my good-looking Uncle Archie, who had tried his hand at modelling and was very charismatic, had a mystique I found intriguing. He even had a wonderful voice that had led to a stint in radio and when it came to women in his life, he'd been married more than once and always seemed to have a gorgeous lady on his arm. He had an air of all-over-the-place and floated all around the country, so he was always in some new location to visit and be fascinated by – especially in my young and impressionable eyes. Coincidentally, he'd also tried his hand at a law degree but then switched things up before finishing and, despite usually being fairly stable, was quite often just plain bat-shit crazy. My parents always referred to him as a bit of an oddball and even as a child, I'd been able to see glimpses into his impulsive and manipulative nature.

But it was when my father and I were visiting him in Sydney one weekend – where we were staying in an amazing apartment my grandfather owned in Kirribilli – that he handed me a copy of *Penthouse*, with its dark seductive colours and incredibly enticing model on the cover. It was a highly inappropriate birthday present for a child but it was one that left an indelible impression on me. As I scuttled off to turn its pages in the privacy of the bathroom, a mental switch turned on. It wasn't something implanted suddenly, and I think he'd recognised that and had chosen it deliberately, to spark some kind of awakening in me that he knew was bubbling beneath the surface, just as it had when he was a child, perhaps.

I became aware of a world I'd already been thinking about subconsciously. Now, my senses tingled with the raw truth of it all. It wasn't long afterwards that my explorations of my own body reached a fever pitch, much to my grandmother's discomfort one day after entering my room unannounced, only to discover me furiously jerking off. I didn't see sex or nudity as anything seedy though. For me, it was incredibly alluring and I couldn't wait to be an adult to experience it. As a child though, my body and mind craved excitement and the consequent rush of sensory pleasure brought on by an orgasm. The way my blood seemed to explode through my veins, the way my brain seemed to be shaken and squeezed and awoken with such a flood of fire and feeling. It felt liberating and became something I began to long for and, as my teenage years progressed, my need to share those feelings with a sexual partner only intensified.

It wasn't until much later – when I was in my late teens – that I was first diagnosed with bipolar. Giving the seismic fluctuations in my moods an official name had its benefits, but it also had its problems. Sure, you have access to the correct medications and you can begin to learn how to live with yourself, but labels can also be powerful things. The idea of being a manic depressive trying to function in a normal society was a self-fulfilling prophecy I was not keen to buy into, but some things were undeniable. Looking back at my high school years, I realised that for me, things were always fully-on, or fully-off. I think I was in year eight when I first smoked weed. But I didn't just dabble. I saved up and had to buy the most expensive setup imaginable to do it properly. A huge bong, with all the bells and whistles. Mum found it one day but didn't say anything. She possibly may have had no idea what on Earth it was, now that I think about it. I wasn't a visible stoner though and I was still pulling off my good kid persona, both at school and at home.

When I indulged in more self-medication and dabbled in drinking – along with every other teenage friend I had – I drank to passed-out excess, and when I got my driver's license, I lost it two short weeks later after I found myself in a booze bus queue. Alcohol and drugs tuned out my insecurities and made me feel more comfortable with myself and the people around me. Or at least that's what I felt. In reality, it made me a laughing stock and somewhat of an exhibit. A crazy fool to be handled in small doses only – particularly when alcohol was involved.

Throughout all of this, the rave scene provided me with the outlet I was looking for. I loved the dancing and the exercise and I loved the music. I craved the feeling of being part of the culture – perhaps even being accepted by the culture – as the drugs loosened my muscles and my mind. I loved to move with the beats and move as one with the crowd as though both were a part of me. I thoroughly enjoyed being out until the normal world began its day and I loved the feeling of belonging to a like-minded community – even if it was for a few drug-fuelled hours every few weeks. Feeling as good as possible for as long as possible was incredibly addictive to me. The alternative was reality – and that just didn't appeal to me.

Chapter 13 – The Birthday Girl

It wasn't unusual for clients to book time with me as a celebration of certain milestones – usually fortieth, fiftieth or even sixtieth birthdays, or sometimes to celebrate new beginnings. On this occasion, my soon-to-be lover had had a tough time leading up to her fiftieth birthday. It was her very good friend who first contacted me, asking if I could be there as her present to my client, Maria. According to the friend, a divorce, losing the house she loved in the financial settlement and having grown kids who had finally left the nest had left Maria all alone with more time on her hands than she'd had in decades.

I was told that she was a busy, interesting woman with a good job and a lot of stuff going on, but her marriage was loveless for many years and they only stuck together for the kids. Maria's friend didn't think she'd had sex for at least five years, maybe even longer.

She told me that Maria tried online dating, but ended up having a disastrous experience with a guy who was so incredibly disrespectful that she vowed to never try it again. Now that she was turning fifty, her friend wanted her to celebrate so she decided to buy her a gift that was sure to put a smile on her face. She told me that she'd booked a room in the city and she wanted me to help her feel spoilt and special for the occasion.

I'd once been summoned to a hotel on the other side of Melbourne – a good hour's drive for me – for a 'surprise' booking that had been arranged by a husband for his wife. After much fluffing around to get the timing right, I knocked on the door of their hotel room. The poor woman inside had no idea what was going on, so answered the door in her pyjamas and with a look of sheer horror. When I mentioned that her husband had bought me for her as a present, she looked really embarrassed, as was I, so I beat a hasty retreat. From that day on, I refused to be a surprise for anyone and on this occasion, I was determined for that not to change. I respectfully made that clear to Maria's friend but she assured me that it wouldn't be an issue this time.

'Trust me, Mitch – we've talked about the idea of having an escort before and she's really into it. We even looked at your website together. She thinks you're hot but the reason I'm stepping in is that I don't think she'll ever build up the courage to book you herself,' she explained. Her reasoning is a common refrain. 'It's because she spent way too long being a selfless mother who constantly put the needs of others before her own. Even though she now has the time to focus on herself, I don't think she could justify spending the money – she'd feel too selfish. But she's done so much for me over the years and I want to give her a present she won't forget.'

Hearing that detailed explanation made me feel better and my excitement started to build. If one of the main reasons I went into this was to make a difference in people's lives, then this sounded like it was going to tick that box in a fun way – and with someone who sounded like they would appreciate the time to be treated like a queen.

When the big day arrived, I found myself paying even more attention than usual to the little details. If this woman really hadn't made love for many years, I was keen to make sure that being with me was absolutely perfect for her. I chose my favourite shirt and Italian suit, and matched them with some nice designer loafers. My watch always added a touch of class and, to complement my vibe of stylish success, I paid extra for one of those fancy Ubers. There's something about spending on a bit of luxury that has a direct effect on my mood and self-confidence when I'm particularly nervous.

The friend was there to meet me in the foyer to handle the check-in process. We went to the room together and I could see that it'd already been set up – complete with a beautiful box of chocolates, a very nice bottle of Pol Roger sitting in an ice bucket and two long champagne flutes. I was relieved when she told me she'd broken the news to Maria that afternoon and, as another wonderful gesture, had shouted her treatments in the hotel spa, where she would be indulged with a full pampering session including waxing, manicure, pedicure – the works. The idea of that excited me as well. I've been lucky enough to have a lot of clients who treat the prospect of seeing me as something special enough that they put great time and effort into their appearance. I'd also had a few clients lately who had taken a much more casual approach – wearing clothes they'd been in all day and with hair that hadn't been washed for ages, wreaking havoc on my stress levels. When you're as anxious as me about meeting new clients, the effort required to be sexy and maintain an erection with someone who doesn't give a shit is immense.

Maria's friend seemed as excited as I was. She told me that, as a safety net, she and her husband had treated themselves to a night in the same hotel and would be having dinner in one of the restaurants nearby. She then gave me a wave goodbye and a reminder to call her if I needed her for any reason. She really was an amazing friend.

About thirty minutes later, I received a text telling me that Maria was downstairs waiting to meet me in the foyer. It's a big ask to come up to a hotel room and meet a man that you've never met before, so I always suggest we meet in public (privacy notwithstanding), where we can celebrate with a few drinks and maybe grab a nice meal together before we go back up to the hotel room for fun. I checked myself in the mirror one last time and had a quick scan around the room to make sure everything was looking fabulous before I stashed a few condoms in strategic places, put my lube within easy reach, dimmed the lights and headed down in the lift. I quickly munched on a breath mint to give me that final burst of confidence and, as I stepped out into the lobby, I immediately recognised Maria from the photo her friend showed me – but she looked even better.

She looked amazing, in fact. She was a gorgeous olive-skinned brunette, with a cute little button nose and strikingly dark brown eyes accentuated by lovely long lashes. She was perched nervously on the edge of the couch, one leg crossed over the other, with polished toenails peeping out from her strappy heels. I rushed up to greet her.

'Hi, how are you?'

For the sake of discretion and to help with nerves, I always like to make it look like my client and I are simply old friends catching up.

'Well, hello there!' She nervously giggled.

I could tell she was relaxing already – as was I. I couldn't wait to be with her.

'Have you got a favourite bar around here?' I asked. I wanted her to feel in control of the situation as much as possible.

'You must be mistaking me for somebody cool.' She laughed.

I suggested that maybe we should just go for a walk to pick one that we liked the look of, but secretly knew exactly where to take her as I'd worked out of that hotel plenty of times. I held my hand out and she slipped her palm into mine as we strolled.

'Your friend was so lovely to talk to,' I said. 'She really cares for you.'

She nodded. 'Yeah, she's amazing. I can't thank her enough,

although I've gotta say, I'm pretty nervous.'

I let go of her hand, gave her a big smile and we shared a long, loving embrace.

'You have nothing to be nervous about, Maria. Let's just start as new friends out for a drink and a good chat, with no expectations at all. We'll go entirely at your pace. Sound good?'

I could feel her tension melt away in my arms.

'Yep. Thanks, Mitch.'

There comes a time in almost every booking where I know that I'm getting along with a client and I feel like I can trust them not to stalk me or reveal my real name to others. As mentioned, I don't like playing a character so, at the earliest possible opportunity, I sometimes ask them if they wouldn't mind calling me Dan. Most clients know that we all use pseudonyms in the industry, so it's not usually an issue for them, but I'm still conscious that it's a strange feeling to all of a sudden know someone by an entirely different name. In Maria's case, I definitely felt she was trustworthy, so I got it out of the way as early as I could.

'Hey Maria, this might sound a bit strange, but could you please possibly call me Dan? It's my real name.'

She smiled. What a relief.

'Of course! Thank you. I was wondering that but I didn't want to ask. You definitely look more like a Dan.'

That out of the way, we chose the bar I always recommend. It had enough of a vibe to seem interesting but didn't have the noise and crowds of the others in the area. We decided that espresso martinis were the perfect match for our mood. They're cool, they look good and the caffeine is great for your stamina.

It's amazing what looking good and feeling good can do for your self-confidence and after the pampering she'd enjoyed earlier that day, I could tell Maria was feeling happy and relaxed. By the time we finished our second drink, it was clear that she felt comfortable with me and from the flirty conversation that had been flowing so easily, I had no doubt that our booking would end up the way we all intended it to. I suggested we grab a small bite to eat, so we went for another wander and selected a tapas bar where we grabbed some wine and a couple of sharing plates.

After about forty-five minutes, we called for the bill and I asked her if there was anything else she'd like to do. She tilted her head and looked up at me from beneath the fringe of her thick dark eyelashes.

'Well... I haven't seen our room, yet...'

We walked back to the room hand-in-hand and, after a quick look around, she excused herself to use the bathroom. I drew the curtains, fired up my trusty Bluetooth speaker and put on a bit of R&B. I also made sure my massage oil and lube were within easy reach of the bed to help everything, and everyone, go smoothly. As she approached the couch, I stood, put one hand around her waist and took her other hand in mine to move her into a slow sort of cuddle-dance. As I pulled her tighter against my chest, I buried my nose into her sweet-smelling hair and we shuffled back and forth on the spot, savouring that wonderful feeling of anticipation. After a minute or two, she tilted her face up to mine and our lips met. Gentle and tentative at first, then firmer, as she let her body remember the affection she'd been missing. She kissed me with the hunger of a woman who hadn't been kissed for a very long time, as my hands moved to feel the shape of her beneath the thin fabric of her beautiful dress.

Things moved quickly despite our attempts to take it slow. Any nerves she had seemed to disappear and I lifted her dress and moved my hands over her underwear to feel her. If it felt like she hadn't been kissed for a while, I got the definite feeling that no one had touched her in that way for even longer. She was already moving with strength and confidence and it was driving me wild. Eventually, I couldn't wait any longer so I guided her to the couch, removed her underwear and gently did my thing to serve her. I was determined to give her the most amazing, memorable experience possible. After a wonderful fifteen minutes or so of mutual oral, she broke away and suggested we move to the bed. The sex was incredible after the long build-up, and the attraction I felt for her was about so much more than her looks. She was funny and sweet, and she was as interested in making me happy as she was about relaxing into her own pleasure. We tried a few different positions and I made an effort to slow myself down so I could last as long as possible for her. When we finally finished, it was in a tangle of sweaty sheets and when I suggested she followed me to the huge double shower, I went down on her again against the tiles. It was super hot and we both loved it.

We were only halfway through the five-hour booking, so the night was still young. I got the impression that Maria was a woman who hadn't been out for a while, so I thought that maybe we could break things up by heading to a few bars. To help us get more in the mood, we finished off the champagne as well as some wine from the minibar and giggled our way down the hall to find the nearest lounge bar. We didn't stay long and when we eventually made it back to the hotel room, she confidently asked for more. We played around again for a while before I let her know that unfortunately, I would soon need to head off.

After so many years in a relationship with the same person, it felt like Maria had fallen into a kind of deep sleep where she had forgotten who she once was. I suspect that, possibly, her ex-husband felt the same. I'm not anti-monogamy by any means, but I do wonder just how many women like Maria are out there – women who know they want something more out of life but can't articulate what it might be until they approach their middle years, the kids move out and they realise it's the touch of a different man. Sometimes, they just need to be reminded.

Maria looked beautifully radiant and content, wrapped in her robe with her hair all messy, and we kissed goodbye. As I headed down to the lobby to call my ride, I wondered what adventure she could look forward to next. On the way home, I received a message from her friend with two simple words:

Thank you.

Maria had texted as well.

I loved tonight. Thank you, beautiful man.

I replied with a kiss emoji and poured myself a drink. I had nothing on the next day and was on my usual post-booking high, a feeling I'm sure many sex workers can relate to. I'd done a great job, I'd made a difference, and I was absolutely flying.

Chapter 14 —
The New Rules

When Sam answered the door that morning, she looked older, as it'd been a while. Her hair was tied back and was much longer than I remembered, with a few cute streaks of grey that weren't visible before. Her eyes still had that beautiful twinkle which made me just want to hold her. They were like a window into the past, where I saw brief glimpses of the excitable and youthful woman she used to be, even though her mind was aging at an increasingly accelerated rate.

Sam was living in the family home full-time now, not only because it was safer for her, but also because her ex-husband was using their apartment in between stays with his girlfriend. It was a much nicer arrangement and it seemed as though Sam was more comfortable there as well. After changing our minds a few times about exactly how we should kick off our booking, we went down to the local café and after about fifteen minutes of wandering the strip of shops, my phone rang. I saw that it was Sam's friend, which was very unusual given how important our privacy was to us.

I answered it and heard an immediate and unmistakable

irritation in her voice. She wanted to know exactly where I'd taken Sam and where exactly we were at that moment. She also instructed me to take her home immediately. I couldn't understand the need for this sudden, unprovoked attack and firmly told her that what we did was none of her business and that the only person I answered to was Sam herself. I wasn't some employee she could boss around and in a less-than-polite tone, told her to back off or I'd just hang up on her. My irritation must have surprised her, as she then calmly explained that with Sam's sense of self, place and time now declining so quickly, if the people around her weren't told what was going on ahead of time, the police would now automatically be called if her carers noticed her missing. It was an arrangement now set in stone and one I had no idea about.

I was taken aback, a little offended, and was glad to know these new rules, but felt compelled to remind her that when Sam was with me, my care for her was so great that she was probably safer with me than anyone else. Sam was fully aware of what we were talking about at that point and told me later that the constant babying frustrated her. I suspected she knew we were breaking the rules that morning but she didn't care less. I'd learned that lapses in judgment were yet another symptom of her disease but didn't think she was at that stage yet. I guess I was wrong. She seemed embarrassed to be constantly treated like a child but at the same time, she was realistic. She'd done her research as well and knew a time would come when she might underestimate her limitations and get herself into serious trouble. Seeing her brilliant, once fiercely independent mind begin to second guess itself just made my heart even heavier and my concern for her future intensified.

After our rushed and undeclared coffee date, we arrived back at her house and she forgot her pin code to enter the building. I rambled on about something or other to give her some time to recall it and thankfully, after a few attempts, she eventually did.

Once we were inside cuddling on her couch, we started talking about our feelings of isolation. She explained to me that she felt as though people around her were just waiting for her to die so they didn't have to worry anymore, whereas I admitted that I was struggling with living alone and felt like my family were slowly leaving my life as well. She leaned in for a hug and instinctively I kissed her forehead and reached out to stroke her hair.

'At least I still have you – for now,' she said.

My answer was firm and, I hoped, reassuring. 'I'm not going anywhere.'

But her concern was more about me.

'I don't want this to be stressful for you,' she said. 'I don't want to be a burden for anyone.'

It's hard to imagine how such a conversation could turn sexual but kind, loving care is a hell of an aphrodisiac for me, and the love we made that day felt like the most passionate and emotionally connected we'd ever had. It also felt like we'd both been naughty and broken the rules, and neither of us gave a damn.

Being naughty was fun but the issue of consent, and what it would look like in the strange relationship that was evolving between us, played regularly on my mind. I didn't know how it would end but I did know that we were both still happy with our relationship. With her life slipping away, holding onto the parts of her she still recognised was important, and if I could help for a bit longer, I would do anything I could to. In between kissing her, I often asked her questions designed to jog her failing memory, which also helped to reassure me that she was still in control of the trajectory of our relationship.

'Do you remember that time when we...?'

'Did you see on the news the other day...?'

'When's your little fella's birthday again?'

Reassuringly, she was still okay. Sam was still with me.

Chapter 15 – The First Timer

I wasn't sure what to expect when a new client emailed to book me for my bare minimum of two hours. The craziness of COVID had a way of making everything seem slightly surreal, after such a long time of not being able to connect with my clients in person. I had just returned to Melbourne after a Sydney tour and was filled with the usual conflicting combination of bravado and nerves on the night we were due to meet. There had been something strangely clinical about the woman's messages and now, because she hadn't taken me up on my offer for some getting-to-know-you chatter in the lead up to our meeting, my anxiety was going into over-drive. All the usual worries began to arise but by then, I was getting pretty good at surrendering to them so I just tried to focus on the present and hoped for the best.

Would she actually turn up?

What would she look like?

Would she like me?

WHAT IF I CAN'T GET IT UP?!

Face masks aren't a great accessory to wear when you meet someone for the first time and especially when that meeting is scheduled to end up with sex. As I entered the lobby, there was only one person there, apart from the staff, so it had to be her.

Although most of her body was hidden beneath a conservative-style dress and most of her face was obscured with a mask, what I could see told me she was probably in her mid-thirties and fair-skinned with amazing, youthful green eyes. She had a stout, petite body like a gymnast and a nervous but kind and friendly voice – despite it being slightly muffled by the mask. Realising that if either of us had COVID, the other soon would as well, I happily tore my mask off and gave her a little peck on the cheek. She then abruptly turned and walked towards the elevator. I sensed that she was really nervous. I followed her up to the room and she'd barely shut the door behind us when she removed her mask and spoke:

'Okay... full disclosure... I have to tell you something.' Her gaze barely left the floor; her embarrassment was obvious. 'I'm a virgin.'

My relief at seeing her beautiful face finally almost distracted me from her declaration. They were not the words I was expecting from a woman of her beauty and age, but the reality of her admission hit me with full force.

This one *really* mattered.

We enjoyed a couple of glasses of the Moët she'd brought with her, which helped with the initial small talk but it wasn't enough to loosen her tension completely. When she finally felt comfortable enough to kiss me, my lips were met with close-mouthed pecks that were dry and guarded, which probably hinted at her inexperience. I knew that my role was to take control and guide her through each moment with gentle patience, but I needed to show her that she was still in charge and my body was hers to explore.

She told me that her reason for holding onto her virginity until she was almost forty had a lot to do with her religious upbringing initially but, as time moved on, there'd been a natural fear growing about her physical and emotional ability to simply let go of all those past constraints. There was a lot of embarrassment, too. She knew that waiting so long had made her unusual and, without a love interest coming her way naturally, she'd been too worried to hit the online dating scene, where a potential partner's reaction to her inexperience was unpredictable and might quite possibly have become unpleasant.

Our relationship with our sexuality and our worries about how we compare to society can cause so much angst. There she was, patiently waiting for 'the one', before finally taking control by choosing me. In her quest for research, she'd read all of my reviews and realised that she needed someone who would be tender, sweet and most importantly, patient. My older age was a bonus for her and now that we were together, she seemed to just want to get it over with. I could definitely understand that, but I had the weight of the moment sitting so heavily on me that I was determined to take the time that was needed to make it truly memorable for her.

I'd barely had time to remove my shoes before we kissed again, far more sensually this time, so, still standing, I moved my hand between her legs, over her underwear and her body moved against it with a steady rhythm. I started to unbutton my white shirt so she could kiss my chest and I led her to the bedroom. With the help of plenty of lube, I slowly slid my finger over her and very slowly inside her but she winced as I tried to work my finger past her hymen. I quickly backed off and moved on to oral, to try and help her to relax and to make the whole exercise less 'medical'. She had a willingness to learn about how to please me, too. But at this point, and as I kissed her stomach, I told her it was all about her, and as my face moved down her body and between her legs, I could feel her grinding against my tongue and lips.

My attitude with oral is that it's me completely submitting to my clients. I'm serving and surrendering to them, and I feel like it's a wonderful way of giving them the feeling of safety and control. It's also a hell of a turn-on for me, too. In this case, she had put her trust in me completely and the honour was so tangible, it felt as if there was three of us in that hotel bed. Her. Me. And the virginity that had bothered her for so long.

Eventually, I suggested that we try to go further, so I put a towel under her and reached for a condom and more lube. She grimaced with pain again when I tried to enter her, so I stopped to make sure she was okay. I thought that perhaps she could shift on top to ride me to regulate everything herself but she told me to just keep going, to literally break through and that she would be okay with that. The idea of causing pain to someone during sex went against everything I believed in but, after some more lubricant, patience and determination, we worked on it together and she eventually gave way. When we finally moved apart, I pulled the blanket over her and told her to ignore any blood. I didn't want that to get in the way of her enjoyment. With a newfound resolve, she encouraged me back inside her so I could keep going until I came. My climax may have been a little more theatrical than usual, but I really wanted her to enjoy the feeling of pleasuring a man – something I have no doubt she'd thought about many times.

After some post-coital cuddling, things became a little awkward. Once she stood up to go to the bathroom, gravity took over and her bleeding became worse. It ended up all over the sheets, it was running down her legs and it was even on the floor. The shock in her face was obvious; I wanted to make as little of the situation as possible, so, I quickly grabbed her a couple of towels for between her legs and suggested she jump in the shower while I sorted things out. As I listened to the sound of the water running, I dabbed the blood off the carpet, flipped over the sheets to cover the stains and started tidying up the room as thoroughly as possible.

'I'm absolutely mortified.'

She was standing in the doorway of the bathroom as she said it, wrapped in a robe. She looked so vulnerable and seemed close to tears so I rushed over to give her a big hug to assure her that I wasn't bothered at all and that it was all perfectly natural and nothing I hadn't seen before – which was the truth. After a while, she relaxed again and the mood lightened significantly. I got the sense that my time was up after a while though, so I slowly started to gather up my belongings to leave.

In our final embrace, she asked me if she was everything I'd hoped for and, of course, I said yes, but my only concern was for her.

Was she really okay? I was almost sure of it.

I imagine this was a huge achievement for her. I hoped that because she now felt closer to her own perception of 'normal', whatever that was, she might feel more comfortable going on a more traditional date with someone, and wouldn't feel stressed about having to admit to something that made her feel so different. But first, she mentioned, she wanted a bit more practice, so I made it clear I would be happy to see her again if she wanted that.

I'll never forget that night. And because I was her first, I knew she wouldn't, either.

To make things as easy for her as possible, I called reception and apologised for a dreadful nosebleed I'd suffered and asked if they would mind leaving some fresh sheets by the door – another little trick I'd used before.

Back at home, after I showered and scrubbed at the droplets of blood that had lodged beneath my fingernails, I sent her a message to check that she felt safe and happy, and to let her know that it was an absolute honour to be part of her special night – and to tell her I thought she was a fun and wonderfully sexy lover.

Sadly, I never had the chance to see her again and all I can assume is that her pillow talk about possible future sexual adventures was aimed at keeping things light to help avoid the thought of never seeing each other again. But don't get me wrong – I completely understand why some clients are one-offs. I'm not cheap as mentioned, but there is, and always will be, a little part of me that wonders if I could've provided a better service somehow or if I'd done or said something wrong. Why did I keep doubting myself like that?

Unfortunately (or perhaps fortunately), I never get to know.

With business booming again after the latest lockdown lifted, my calendar was showing six bookings in the next nine days, so I needed to take some time to apply my own self-care – something I seemed good at advising others to do, but was rarely good at in my own life. In theory, it sounded perfectly reasonable and achievable to read a book or meditate, but because I could never get to sleep easily, especially after a booking, I slipped on my Ugg boots, reached for the bottle of vodka I had in my freezer and poured myself a quick drink to calm my thoughts and to let my own version of self-care begin.

Chapter 16 – My First Time

As far as my virginity was concerned, for a boy who had such a rampant appetite for masturbation, soft porn centrefolds and erotic literature, I was a pretty late bloomer when it came to my first time. I met my first-ever lover on the train I used to take to school. I was at Melbourne High (how I snuck into a selective school I'll never know), while she went to an all-girls school in the bayside area. Looking back, not only did she have her youthful beauty with lovely long blonde hair and a mischievous smile, but she was also just... cool. A girl I could completely relax with during that particularly awkward stage of adolescence. We'd had a few dates where we'd meet in nightclubs after successfully gaining entry using pretty legitimate-looking fake IDs, as well as chats over the phone and on the way to school on the train. But on the night of my eighteenth birthday, we both decided to mark the auspicious occasion by having sex, which was made all the more wonderful by her being one of my best friends as well as my girlfriend. In hindsight, the experience spoilt me. Sex with a bestie is the best sex ever. Being in my parents' bed with drunken, rowdy mates celebrating in the next room wasn't particularly romantic, but in the heat of the moment it felt like we were the only two people on the planet. I remember being inside her and feeling her body around me and wondering how this could be any more beautiful, and how incredibly lucky I was.

Despite the frenzied nature of our 'lovemaking' that night, I remember it as the absolute pinnacle of human connection. Someone you cared deeply about and laughed with, joined as one, as the heat of our two bodies mixed together. Looking back, it's similar to when you try a drug for the first time and it absolutely blows your mind to the point where you're always chasing that experience again – for the rest of your life. I think I'm always longing for that depth when I'm intimate with a woman. Longing for that connection. Always on the quest to go further or deeper, and to feel more.

My beautiful first love tragically passed away only a few years later. She was only in her twenties and the news she'd succumbed to breast cancer hit me hard. If that hadn't happened, I have no doubt she would've remained a good friend and I still think about her all the time. By creating Mitch, it felt as though I had given myself an explorer's license that regular life didn't give me, and perhaps it provided a way for me to chase that first sexual high. I felt like a pioneer who was lucky enough to experience emotions and generate feelings with many women, in a world that traditionally accepted being with only one other partner. But what would I ultimately find? Maybe it would just be the real me. But maybe, as a result, that would lead to the happiness I was always looking for.

Chapter 17 –
The Reveal – First Attempt

How do you tell your parents that you're working as a male escort and selling your mind and body for money? It's a question I'd been asking myself a lot lately and I still didn't know the answer. It's not like there was any precedent to it. There were no 'five steps to telling your parents you're a whore' articles on the internet. This one I had to work out on my own. My parents were still struggling to come to terms with the dissolution of my marriage and they still had no idea why it had all fallen apart. It was a few weeks earlier that my wife and I had finally agreed that it was time for me to move out. What we'd both thought was a bit of a side hustle had unexpectedly morphed into me becoming one of the most in-demand male escorts around. I'd been working at least three nights a week for most of the year and when I wasn't sleeping in, I was busy answering and following up on enquiries. I felt like a terrible husband and father, so we agreed that it was time I ventured out on my own for the first time in almost ten years.

It hurt and I was scared but it had to be done.

It felt like my little family of three had become two, and I hated myself for sabotaging our marriage. But once that decision was made, there was no turning back. I had to suck it up on my own and trust that the three of us would be okay.

My parents rightly blamed me and thought that perhaps I'd cheated with some other woman. In a way, they were right. But they were still very wrong. I hated having secrets between us and I was proud of what I was doing. Deciding to be a sex worker for a living had been a revelation to me and at my age, I felt like I was breaking the mould of the typical middle-aged man like never before. Yes, it made me anxious and clearly on the fringe of normality, but when it was good, it was amazing. It felt like I'd finally found something I had a natural talent for, while also doing some good for once.

That didn't mean that I thought I was only good in bed and nothing else, because the reality of what I did as an escort was about so much more. I knew I was making women happy, and that sometimes it was temporary – even if I wasn't always happy myself. The stereotypical vision of a male escort who services women is a sexy one – only gorgeous women and every guy's fantasy of accessing as much sex as he could dream of. That was never my motivation, though, believe it or not. I had a strong need to love and care for people and if that involved sex, then all the better, because I loved that too. What I didn't realise, though, was that the reality of dealing in emotions for a living was all-consuming. There were extreme highs, but equally, there were extreme lows.

Standing in front of a frumpy woman who was wearing tracksuit pants and thongs, and feeling obliged to tell her how horny you felt, was an exhausting role-play, but I was happy to balance it in between those other moments, the amazing opportunities that saw me slide between the sheets with some wonderful women who became not just lovers, but teachers and friends as well. When my clients connected to the Mitch in me, Dan felt good by osmosis. Seeing Mitch make a difference for the women who paid for his company was better than any anti-depressant I'd ever been prescribed, even if I still did experience those hollow, in-between crashes. But feeling good about what I did never really made it any easier to reveal to my parents the truth of what I'd actually been up to since leaving law, photography and my marriage. I rehearsed the conversation in my head many times but the butterflies in my belly only flapped faster and more furiously.

I remember turning up at their house for lunch and to mow their lawn one afternoon while Mum fussed about, cleaning the kitchen. In my head, my voice sounded so clear:

Mum... Dad... Can we have a quick chat?

But that voice never made it to my mouth. I wheeled the mower back to the shed and washed my hands at the kitchen sink before I pulled up a chair at the dining table. I listened to their stories about friends of theirs or the latest news and just knew it wasn't the right time. I couldn't just drop it on them like that. I nodded politely before accepting Mum's offer of another coffee before I hugged them goodbye. I really did have something I needed to tell them and it was burning a hole in my heart, but not that day.

Chapter 18 – The Toy Lover

Going to this particular client's bookings meant ticking an extra couple of jobs off my usual preparation routine. Yes, I'd had a shower and my clothes were clean. My waxing, shaving and plucking were all on-point, and of course, my breath was fresh and my hair smelled nice, but this client had a special passion – sex toys. As a result, my day was made busier by making sure my equipment had been freshly and thoroughly sterilised, charged and ready for action. I'd packed the chargers for the ones that might need them, along with lube, condoms and baby wipes – everything an escort could possibly need to please a woman, along with my carefully chosen tools of the trade.

She was a little pocket rocket and lots of fun. She was really short, but that turned me on – especially when she wore the high heels, pencil skirt and blazer she strutted around in at work. Whenever we cuddled, she always liked to bury her face in my chest and loved it when I completely enclosed her in my arms and stroked her hair. She was a junior barrister with a wonderful lust for life and I loved the chats we had about the legal system and the various briefs she'd received. I really admired how she stayed so positive and enthusiastic whilst working in what I'd known to be such a high pressured and often very unpleasant industry. Our conversations weren't always one-sided though, and she always asked me all sorts of questions about my line of work, with what seemed like genuine interest.

After our initial kisses and cuddles, we didn't waste time. We'd usually pour ourselves a drink and move into the bedroom before I'd start peeling her clothes off. On many occasions, once she was down to her underwear, I liked to spice things up by placing a blindfold over her eyes before proceeding to completely undress her. And then the real fun would start.

I sometimes liked to begin with chopsticks. Regular old wooden chopsticks. They could be used softly or with more pressure, could be very precise and were a great way to get the nerves of the inner thigh firing – especially when combined with some very gentle, almost imperceptible strokes of my tongue. Another great little device I liked to use early on was a buzzing little bean-shaped thing that I'd slowly slip inside her. This was sometimes accompanied by my medium-sized butt plug – although fair warning had to be given before that happened, of course. If she seemed particularly keen, I'd sometimes use my sonic soundwave clitoral stimulator – better known as a 'Womanizer'. That one wasn't for the faint-hearted, though, so I always made sure it was on its lowest setting and I introduced it very slowly. She loved to feel my mouth on her nipples while all of this was going on so I often found myself kneeling over her with my teeth nibbling one nipple, then the other, as one hand held the Womanizer steady over or around her clit, while the weight of that same hand pushed her groin down against the bean-shaped thing inside her.

If all this sounds complicated, it's because it was. I often felt like a DJ – spinning decks, tweaking knobs and pushing sliders – to build the anticipation before eventually dropping the beat to the crowd – but in this case, I was working my crowd of one up to an intense orgasm. She loved oral as well, but I liked to mix the pressure of my tongue with the harder buzzing of another vibrator. That's when I would slowly remove the bean-shaped one and insert the slightly larger vibrator – sometimes in replacement of the butt plug.

I rarely felt as though I was missing out, though, as we absolutely adored kissing each other whenever physically possible and she always liked to hold onto my cock to encourage me along as her body writhed sensually on the bed. She was amazingly in tune with her body, and often came many times – and always nice and loud – but occasionally, a part of me did feel a bit redundant. I once asked her why she paid me when, for the investment of a few hundred dollars, she could go out and buy all the equipment she would ever need – with no man required.

'It just wouldn't be the same without you,' was her reply.

Her encouragement always inspired me to try even harder, so I would often try twisting and turning my tools in new ways while watching her carefully to gauge her reaction.

It often felt like a bit of an afterthought to include actual penetrative sex but sometimes, when she was blindfolded, I'd put myself inside her and it would drive her wild.

One last little ritual that I really loved was that when our time was up, she always reached for her phone, opened her calendar and appeared almost desperate to secure another booking with me. More often than not, I'd have a look at my own schedule and tell her we were good to go, and we'd lock it in. I would then stow my equipment in individual sandwich bags before stowing them inside the unassuming plain backpack I brought them in for the trip home. The following morning, I would thoroughly clean and sterilise them and make sure they were charged and ready for next time. I would usually need a recharge, too. Although she made me feel like I was the only one who could navigate her body with the toys I provided, in the exact way that satisfied her, I usually left that client feeling kind of used. It was a strange feeling but, as I tried to see it, at least I'd made someone happy.

And that was exactly what kept me going.

Chapter 19 – The Student

I'd spoken with this particular new client several times on the phone. She was very laid-back and easy to chat with, so I didn't mind a few free phone calls leading up to the booking. She was another one who was interested in toys, so we agreed to meet up in the car park out the front of *Sexyland* so she could pick something out. It was her first time with an escort and she'd booked a motel room not too much further down the road. Sadly, it was one of those cheaper, depressing little places that dot outer suburban highways but I didn't mind as I already felt at ease with her after our many conversations – and above all, she sounded quite attractive.

She said she wanted to stretch her sexual wings by experiencing what it would be like to be with another man and she'd been honest with me about her circumstances. She was married, with two kids at school and during the day she spent her time running pilates classes, whilst also doing some of the book-keeping at her husband's medical practice. She'd met her husband in high school and still thought him a sweetheart, despite the fact he'd cheated on her some three years prior. She only found out a year ago, while on a family holiday in Bali. He was eventually forced to come clean when his colleague – the person he'd slept with (and several times, mind you) – started contacting him again after many months of silence. The husband, according to my client, claimed that he was going through an emotionally turbulent time, wasn't thinking clearly and, as I've heard so many times before, sank into a deep depression when found out. All this conveniently forced my client into a caring, compassionate role that robbed her of her right to express her anger. I bit my tongue when I heard this, to hide my contempt; I just listened and acknowledged – as I'd learned to do. I'd heard similar stories before and I guarantee I'll hear them again. A few months after my client found out, she started following me on Twitter and Instagram as her desires, as well as her resentment, grew. She said she felt no remorse whatsoever for what was about to happen and I could tell from the moment we first spoke that she was being truthful, and was committed.

Last year, her best friend left her husband after he, too, had an affair – but my client wasn't ready to leave her husband – yet. To pay for our time together (and for the toys she wanted to buy), my client used some cash that she had been squirrelling away for herself. We had to slot it in between 11 am and 2 pm so she had time to go and pick up her kids afterwards, which was great, as it allowed for a little bit of overtime and it gave me the night off.

Meeting up at the adult store gave the booking a wonderfully light and fun feeling that wasn't conducive to any talk of her husband's infidelity. I got the impression that she just wanted me to show her a good time. She was curious about how her own body might enjoy new ways of being pleasured and to her credit, she said she also wanted to learn how better to please a man. I assumed she was talking about her husband, but I secretly hoped not.

It was a gorgeous day and when I saw her standing next to a shiny little white BMW, I felt an immediate sense of relief. She was a naturally cute-looking sun-kissed blonde with cheeky dimples and a smattering of freckles across her nose. She looked like the type that worked hard in the gym and might've skied in the winter: she was tanned, wealthy and had a beautifully toned body. I'd dressed more casually for the occasion – jeans and a pale blue t-shirt, while she looked just scrumptious in white jeans, high heels and a close-fitting light pink blouse.

'Shall we head in?' I suggested.

I guided her through the doors and we headed straight to the wall of vibrators. I was glad she'd chosen this particular shop because, although I was familiar with the Sexyland chain, I'd never been to this exact store and I didn't want the staff greeting me with too much friendly familiarity. The last thing I wanted was for my client to feel as though she was just one in a long list of people I'd done this with before. Making the decision to book an escort and paying good money to extract some of my experience and expertise is one thing, but getting the feeling that this was just another job for me was entirely another. When you work as a sex worker, being organised and business-like needs to be balanced with your ability to make your clients feel like there's something special about what you're doing with them, as if it's the very first time. I was aware of her time limits and after some browsing and giggling, we took a few goodies to the counter so she could pay for them.

We'd agreed to travel to the motel in separate cars and, as she indicated out onto the main road, I followed her to the car park. She was still nervous but the ice had been broken in a way that only buying a vibrator together could do. Years of dealing with patients, suppliers and staff at her husband's practice had given her a particular attitude to time management and because she knew that she was there for a reason, she quickly cut to the chase.

'I want to know how to give better head, for starters.'

I told her that I could definitely help her with that, but that first I wanted her to enjoy herself. I started with a light shoulder massage to get her into the mood. We then started kissing and I moved my hands to grab her wonderful butt. I asked if I could give her a proper massage, as I was incredibly turned on by her body at that stage. She removed her blouse, jeans and bra and I had a wonderful time spreading my massage oil all over her – and in her. While I played with her, I changed the speed and the intensity and used my fingers and tongue to help her along and at one point, based on the pressure I felt building up within her, I realised I could make her squirt if she wanted to. Squirting remains a bit of a mystery for me. Some women can do it, while others can't. Some claim to come when they squirt, whereas others describe it as a sort of 'release' which is totally different to an orgasm. On this occasion, my client laid back afterwards looking amazed at what she'd just done. It was a really cool party trick and I loved seeing how much fun she was having already. The sheets were already completely destroyed, of course, but neither of us cared.

I lay down on the bed next to her and was relieved that I was still rock hard for her blowjob lesson. I shared a few tips that worked for me and I let her know that she was doing a fantastic job.

Forget what you've seen in porn.

Very little deepthroating.

Think of it like sucking the tip of an ice cream.

Don't neglect the balls.

No teeth!

She was a fast learner and by the time the booking was up, we'd managed to cover lots of different ways she could put a smile on her next lucky partner's face while always making sure her own needs were met. That's what really matters. It's not about how happy you can make him. You have to feel happy yourself and then you'll be ready to make him happy, too. I'm no sex therapist, but she seemed to think I was making sense. After a timeless couple of hours, she snuck a glance at her phone and realised that she needed to get going. We shared a very passionate kiss farewell and as I hopped into my car, I watched her walk towards the hotel reception to return the key. She was brimming with confidence as she carried her bag of toys to take home to her husband. I hadn't used them on her in the end, because not only was it not the right situation but I also thought that it might somehow take away the excitement of breaking them in with her husband – assuming he was fortunate enough to see them.

Although she was feeling fine about the booking when I left her, I had a feeling there would be a part of her that struggled with the guilt of keeping her secret from him and that she'd probably tell him the truth one day. I really hoped that it wouldn't make anything more difficult for her but from experience, I knew it would. There would be the usual initial shock; her husband would play the victim again and they'd have a little honeymoon period where everything would be great, including the sex, but then it would all slowly unravel. I think that ultimately though, she would come out the other side feeling proud, independent and strong. I thought there would be a lot of pain in the meantime though, sadly. As I've mentioned, I remain in contact with many women well after I've seen them professionally and I hear of what transpires. But this includes the good stuff, too. Once they've been out on their own for a while, I usually get a few messages telling me all about their new partners or the amazing things they are doing on their own, but then their messages drop off and eventually cease altogether as I become a distant memory. It hurts a bit, but I recognise that it's the best possible outcome and I consider it maybe even be a little pat on the back for me.

Once again, though, I found myself feeling alone and empty that afternoon, so I met one of my friends for a quick drink in Acland Street, St Kilda. Over coffee, I asked her how her own business was going and she told me it was better than ever. The effects of the pandemic were still having a huge impact on some industries, but for ours, it seemed that the prolonged periods of being unable to see people you cared about created a unique kind of frustration which meant busy business as the country reopened. People had been lonely and Lord knows I was one of them. I was glad activity was picking up, I told my friend – but it hadn't helped my own mental state. It actually felt as though it had got worse. We both spoke of the difficulties of finding and holding onto love when your daily working life included sex with random strangers or intimate attachments with regulars. After the fun of that day, the idea of a relationship seemed way too complex and hard to manage, so I just continued to stumble along, alone.

Chapter 20 – Starting to Slip

It's the stuff that happened in between the bookings that made me think of her. From the first time I met her, we fell into an easy habit of ringing or texting each other every couple of days. It was something I did with a lot of my regular clients to stay connected but with Sam, it seemed more important. I could tell that she liked the sound of another voice to help her break up her lonely days and I liked to know how she was coping mentally. It kind of felt like the least I could do.

Sometimes, we spent too much time talking about the weather, but just when I thought I might've been boring her, I imagined her, maybe in the little garden in her front yard, watching the world around her, as active people out on the street did active things, and it reminded me that it was the stuff we took for granted that often mattered the most.

If Sam was having a bad day, she'd talk to me about the fear that gripped her and I would just listen and acknowledge what she was going through, without pretending to understand. I wanted her to know I was always there for her and that by talking about the disease, we might have some chance at keeping each other positive and still looking to the future – even though we both knew there was little to look forward to. If it was cancer that was threatening her future, we could be talking about chemotherapy or experimental treatments and the chances she might've had for survival. But based on what I'd read, I knew that what was happening to her didn't offer any real hope, and *that* reality added a heaviness to my soul which made it hard to keep smiling.

I'd read about the way people with Alzheimer's could forget the most mundane words and so I looked out for any clues that Sam was struggling. Although her speech occasionally stopped mid-sentence, as if she needed a moment to grab the right word, nothing appeared to have completely left her vocabulary yet, thankfully.

She texted me again, obviously alone and clamouring for some comfort. Her filter had dropped away even further, however. In one sentence she might share with me how scared she felt, then in the next, she'd tell me how horny she was. I was constantly reminded of the confusion that was now a part of me and the way the heaviness of the world always found a way to burrow deeply under my skin. I wasn't sure how to respond to her texts, so I replied with a simple 'goodnight' with the obligatory heart emoji and told her that I was catching an early night's sleep ahead of a big day with my boy. But the truth was that I was at home alone with no plans, so I decided to follow up a fat line of coke with some vodka on ice. I welcomed the familiar numbness in my nostrils as I waited for the various substances to weave their magic on my shattered spirit to take me away from myself.

Chapter 21 – Christy

Every client I met had a story. Some I got snippets of during one-off bookings, whereas others revealed more about their complex histories as our relationship progressed. Christy was one of those. She didn't speak much at all and was initially quite guarded, but after a while, I learned all about what she'd been through. Her ex-husband, I discovered, was a complete and utter flaming arsehole. He was an alcoholic – which I was certainly in no position to judge, but the fact that he was physically and verbally abusive as well showed that he was weak and an absolute insult to men everywhere.

She was a very tall, full-figured woman in her late forties, with her straight blonde hair styled into a bob and a cute fringe that just covered her eyebrows. From the second we first met, I could tell that she wasn't the type to take shit from anyone. She worked in sales, and I imagined her being a pretty ruthless manager who expected good results from her team and didn't tolerate excuses. She was certainly intimidating, but that just made her all the more alluring to me. Her decision to contact me was about wanting to reconnect with men but in a safe environment. As with many other people I'd met, she'd given internet dating a go but it didn't go well at all for her. After being subjected to the usual disparaging comments from anonymous nobodies, she finally went on a date. Disappointingly, the man she met lacked any sort of manners and became irritated when she made it clear that she didn't want to have sex with him in the back of his car, minutes after they'd first met, in the carpark of the restaurant they were about to visit. I just shook my head when I heard this and wondered what sort of an upbringing can produce a person with so little regard for other people? As a result, her already almost non-existent self-esteem took another big hit. So much so, that when she first contacted me, she had such little confidence that I found it difficult to persuade her that I was genuinely happy to see her as my client. She was convinced I was doing her a huge favour and I remember spending many frustrating moments in the early days continually reassuring her that I really, honestly did want to be with her. Helping her rediscover her self-esteem and restoring her faith in men, I realised, was exactly what she needed me for.

Christy originally contacted me purely for non-sexual social dates, and each week we would take turns choosing a restaurant roughly halfway between us so that we could get to know each other better. It felt like she was keen for some male company but wasn't ready to take the plunge by asking for anything more intimate – which was understandable and quite common. After our fourth dinner, however, and just after we'd hugged and kissed each other goodbye, she asked me if I'd like to join her for a weekend away in the Yarra Valley wine region. It was a big step for her and quite a long booking for me, so I was a bit nervous, and I could tell she felt the same way – but we needn't have worried. We had a magical time. It was wonderful seeing her laugh and it was a pleasure showering her in affection and generally treating her like a queen. I could tell it was a nice escape for her and I hoped I was bearing witness to a new, happier chapter in her life. I got the impression that she longed for intimacy but that it came with negative connotations, given her husband's behaviour over the years. I hoped that by booking me, she might've become just a little bit more receptive to the idea that she could feel beautiful, free and confident again, and maybe even venture back out into the dating world.

When we made love that weekend, I felt a huge release within her, and the emotions she displayed were like nothing I've ever witnessed before or since. She became almost primal during sex and it was unbelievably hot. She loved raking her fingernails across my back in the throes of ecstasy and, as she twitched and orgasmed with me inside her, she would dig them into my flesh. It felt incredible. That amazing transformation during sex and the satisfied, blissful smile she always had afterwards, made me feel incredibly valued and was another reminder of why I loved doing what I did.

It was still early in our relationship and I could sense a big shift in its intensity that weekend. We'd seen each other many times already, of course, but the bond we formed over those two days was an indication that things had the potential to become very serious, very quickly. Christy was a hard, resilient woman – seemingly conditioned to guard her emotions – but that weekend it felt as though she was finally opening up and emerging from her chrysalis. Eventually, though, we would have to accept that she needed to continue her journey alone. The last thing I wanted was for her to feel that the tenderness I'd shown her was just an act or solely just 'work' for me. I wanted her to see herself as I did – as a kind, loving and confident woman who deserved happiness and respect. I wanted her to know that love was abundant and that she would eventually find it in whatever form she desired. But perhaps I've always just believed it should be abundant.

I always was a bit of a romantic, I suppose...

Chapter 22 — Fun In the Park

Sam wanted a social date that day. I'm not sure if that was for financial reasons, whether her carers made the decision, or if it was just companionship she felt like – but a social date it was. She was always a bit of a thrill-seeker, so this time she asked to be taken for a spin on my motorbike. I was initially a bit worried about her ability to hold on tightly but remembered that her disability affected her mind at this stage – not her body – and as it turned out, she was just fine.

We took a ride along the beach from Port Melbourne to Black Rock, which was always a favourite of mine – easy, slow and relaxing for my passengers, and never too far from my place in St Kilda. I kept the speed down and could tell by her frequent giggles that the open air and vibrations of the Harley were making her excited. I'd been looking things up online again and had read that for many people with Alzheimer's, there could be a dramatic impact on that person's inhibitions, their sexual behaviour and that it could even affect their creativity. Sexual interest could be displayed in a direct, open way with no inhibitions and in Sam's case, this was definitely true. Despite being privy to some of her most intimate aspects, I still didn't know how her illness would affect her so, at that stage, I was cautious about how I reacted to her sexually. Clear consent was essential – as it was with all clients – but in Sam's case, it required more attention and frequent check-ins. I didn't want to appear overly cautious though, as that would take away a lot of the fun for both of us, and my impression of her pre-diagnosis persona was that she was a vibrant, confident and highly sexual woman anyway. Even though her illness was slowly dismantling her sexual energy, I still saw glimpses of her need for variety and excitement – to the point where she would openly ask to experiment with something new – and that day served as a good example.

We'd pulled over in a secluded area of a car park in Elwood and were both sitting on the grass enjoying the sunshine when I noticed Sam staring at me with a cheeky, lopsided grin on her face. I asked her what was so amusing and she replied:

'You look fucking hot, Dan. I want you in my mouth right here. Right now.'

I just laughed it off but when she leaned back, unbuttoned her jeans, took hold of my hand and put it down her underwear to show me how wet she was, it became clear she was serious. I'd always been a pretty spontaneous sort of guy and have had sex in public before, but her request came out of nowhere and I was immediately concerned about whether it was Sam or the Alzheimer's talking. In the end, I felt like I didn't have much say in the matter as we stood up and started to kiss. There was no one around; there was a lovely and warm coastal breeze blowing and the naughtiness of what we were about to do made me rock hard, so we went behind the nearest big tree and she gave me some of the most amazing oral sex I've experienced. I can count the number of times I've come from oral sex on one hand and that was one of them. It was such a heavenly and impromptu surprise – made even sexier given the risk of being caught.

That whole day was amazing but the blunt way in which she practically demanded sex reminded me that her empathy was something that would be impaired further as her illness progressed. Being with Sam felt liberating in many ways, but at other times, it could seem almost workman-like – as if her body craved certain sensations but her mind had forgotten how to encourage and invite them respectfully. With Sam, it didn't bother me as much – as it might have with another client – as I knew it was the disease talking, not the kind and beautiful woman underneath.

The 'coffee only' status of that day had obviously gone out the window, but I would never be so crass as to ask for more money. It was fun for both of us and it was a nice break from the doom and gloom conversations we'd been having recently. As our time came to a close, I rode her back home, walked her to the door, made sure she remembered her pin code and saw her safely into her house. At the door, I leaned in for a kiss and she seemed surprised at first – as if she'd forgotten what we had just done – but eventually, she passionately kissed me back and it felt as tender as always. As I fired up the bike to head back home that day, all I could do was shake my head and think: *Just another day at the office...*

Chapter 23 – The Mature One

If someone had told me that I'd end up having sex with somebody old enough to be my mother, I don't think I'd have believed them.

In my regular life, I have a 'type', and most of my girlfriends along the way have fitted the bill. I can see beauty in lots of women but I've always had a soft spot for women with long, thick hair and nice skin, and I'm a sucker for kind, beautiful eyes. I think curves are voluptuous and gorgeous, and, as someone who tries to keep my own body in some sort of decent shape, I do especially like women who maintain their own levels of fitness too. When it comes to age, though, as an officially middle-aged guy, I find myself attracted to women close to my age or slightly older and find that sleeping with anyone in their twenties can feel borderline inappropriate. Analysing my thoughts about how much older a woman would have to be before I saw her as off-limits was never something I thought too much about. If I hooked up with someone on Tinder who turned out to be a few years older than me, I wouldn't blink an eye. I mean, why should I? But would I ever actively seek out and date a seventy-year-old?

Well… no.

So, when I got a text from a potential client whose first question to me was about whether or not I had a cut-off for age, I felt my heart miss a beat before I gulped and tentatively replied:

Of course not! May I ask how old you are?

I wasn't stunned as such but more intrigued by her reply.

I'm seventy-two.

I wasn't quite sure what response was appropriate so I just kept it honest.

I'm sure you are absolutely beautiful.

She told me that she was looking for a relationship with an escort she could trust, who was as close as possible to her own age but not completely over the hill in the bedroom. She explained to me that her husband had recently passed away and she desperately missed the feeling of a man's presence in her bed and in her life. She dangled the carrot of interstate trips (she was in Perth), overnight bookings and, sometimes, shorter dates as she passed through Melbourne for business.

As I've mentioned, for an escort to have any sort of long-term success, it's vital to build up a base of regular clients. With regulars, however, there was an emotional trade-off in lots of ways and the giving of a service could wind up feeling like it was giving so much more of your real self. The benefits included the financial security of guaranteed bookings and less stress in general about who you were about to meet. Regular sex could be more rewarding for both me and the client, as familiarity brought its own unique knowledge of each other's pleasure points and sexual preferences. Conversely, of course, that familiarity could also breed the sort of dynamics more associated with married couples if things aren't kept sexy and interesting. But with a 72-year-old? What would that bring? I thought about my business goals and how I planned to work for as long as possible, and wondered if that meant that I would eventually be having sex with someone who was almost eighty. But then I slowed myself down and realised I was jumping the gun and overthinking things, as usual.

She told me that she was a successful business owner and that she reluctantly now controlled a construction company her recently deceased husband had founded in the eighties. She said she'd only seen herself in the supportive wife role for the past forty-odd years and that the situation she now found herself in had reawakened sexual urges she had no idea she still had. I then asked her approximately when she would like to meet me, to which she replied with a confidence I've come to associate with older women, 'The sooner, the better. When can you fly over?'

It was new territory for me and after we'd settled on the logistics of our first booking, I felt a kind of panic rise up as I started to worry about the potential downfalls. What if the huge age gap meant we had nothing in common to talk about? What if she reminded me of my mother? Calming myself down a bit, I put the date, time and address in my calendar and reminded myself that I was a professional and that all would be okay. It was a big job worth big money and it was a chance to meet a woman who sounded like she'd lived an intriguing, impressive life. For me, the attraction was never just about the physical, although I'd be a liar if I pretended it didn't make a difference. Conversation can be a powerful aphrodisiac and, from what we'd chatted about on the obligatory pre-booking phone call, I knew that she wouldn't be the type to run out of stories. I decided to stop thinking too much about it and convinced myself that, even if it didn't turn into an ongoing booking, it would still be an adventure. Something to tick off my bucket list. That said, having sex with a 72-year-old was never actually on my bucket list to begin with but, hey, now it was, and I was on the cusp of fulfilling that previously unrequired goal. I wondered what my estranged wife would think, but I decided not to tell her until after the event – if at all. I was positive my parents would never understand, either. But that was okay – they were completely oblivious about everything at that point, anyway.

We planned to meet for dinner in one of the nicer Italian restaurants in town before heading back to her house, where I would stay with her overnight. I flew in early and had a few hours to kill, so I booked a room at a backpacker's hostel to give me somewhere to prepare while also saving me a few bucks. That was actually quite an unexpectedly fun afternoon, which culminated in me regaling a few of the travellers with stories about work over a few beers. My anxiety levels had hit new heights, though – and even adhering to my rituals of waxing, gym work and a cheeky sniff of pretty average white powder I'd procured in the hostel did nothing to calm me down. It was, after all, a big ask to fly to the other side of the continent to spend the whole night with a much older woman who was also a total stranger. I knew she would be a strong woman who wouldn't suffer fools gladly so my conversation skills also needed to be at their best. When we finally met, it was very reassuring to see she took pride in her appearance and had an air of confidence about her – and that was all I needed to start getting interested.

I would never say such a thing of course, but she did look in her seventies. She was quite short, stood slightly stooped and had thinning, curly dark hair that fell just below her shoulders in a very age-appropriate way. The clothes she wore were classily understated, and a sneaky look at the labels during dinner revealed that they were very expensive. Our conversation eventually became very easy and very relaxed. I could tell that she was quite nervous to start with by the way she repeatedly filled in the gaps of our conversation with graphic stories about her husband's illness, only to then correct herself for doing so. I didn't mind at all, as it was clear that she was still coming to terms with what she was doing, what was about to happen, and the fact that it wasn't with her husband of almost fifty years.

We eventually finished our dinner and she called her driver to take us home. Before we hopped into the car, she made it clear to me that he was not to be made aware of the nature of our relationship. I was a friend she'd met at her dancing group and that was the story I was to stick to. I felt slightly offended, not only because this suggested I was someone she was ashamed of being with but also because I was a professional and I automatically assumed that secrecy was expected at all times. Once we arrived at her place, however, and after we'd taken off our shoes and coats and poured some drinks, I began to relax. She lived in a lovely area of town, in a modern but cozy little house suited to an older lady living alone. Her minimalist decor indicated to me that she had possibly even moved in recently after the loss of her husband. I felt welcome and surprisingly comfortable though. After a couple of hours of talking and slow dancing, I could tell it was time for me to help her make the leap, so I suggested that perhaps we could go to her bedroom where I could start by giving her a head and shoulder massage. So as not to be awkward, I reached out and held her for a while before I gently kissed her. She was so nervous and felt so fragile, our lips barely touched. I didn't expect that we would make love any time soon (if at all), but just wanted her to slowly become comfortable with being close to me – this man who wasn't her husband.

We moved to the bedroom and lay on her bed together, both lying on our backs but with her head on my stomach, which allowed me to stroke her hair and massage her temples and shoulders. She was strictly a lights-off woman, which is never my preference, but with her, I could understand. It had been twelve years since she'd made love due to her husband's health issues and several decades since she'd been with another man – and she was understandably petrified. Beneath my fingers, I could feel the softness of her skin. It was fine, like thin cotton, but in a beautifully feminine way. As I gently massaged her shoulders and back, I could feel her skin mould against my hand, then just as easily slip away from my grasp in a way that seemed delicate and precious. I see beauty in all different shapes and sizes and in my client's case, a lot of her beauty came from the strength and resilience she'd shown as a widow forced to inherit the resposibility of running a huge company in an industry that was completely dominated by men. There was a definite sense that this lady wouldn't put up with bullshit and I quickly made my mind up not to give her any. I believe that's why we hit it off straight away and why she eventually trusted me with her near-naked body. We both knew that there was a huge age gap and we were under no illusions about the transactional nature of our relationship. She asked me how often I was tested for STIs, whether I slept with men or couples and whether I ever had unprotected sex. All of which I answered truthfully.

When the time was right for her and we finally made love, it was very slow going as I was being very careful not to hurt her. Being in total darkness and being almost silent made the whole experience feel slightly disjointed to me, but I suspect that's how she wanted it to be out of respect for her husband. Nevertheless, she had a certain level of confidence and knowledge of her own body that was alluring and I followed her lead and focused on what her body responded to in order to satisfy her. It worked, but a part of me was already wondering how much I wanted it to work again.

At the end of our booking, she told me that she definitely wanted to see me again and when she asked about my willingness to travel interstate again, I found myself nodding and smiling and telling her that I was quite happy to. In those early days in the job, I found myself saying all sorts of things that surprised me and I often wondered – was I evolving as an escort?

Or was I devolving into a guy who would do anything for money?

Chapter 24 –
My Daddy The Gigolo

Could I be a sex worker and still be a good parent? If I tuned into talkback radio to listen to such a debate, I'd probably walk away feeling shit about everything I did. But I still felt proud. I tried to be a good father to my son and my work didn't change that. Okay, so the drugs weren't great, but show me a person with bipolar who'd never self-medicated to some degree and I'll show you a liar. And I never used anything on the days and nights I was with my boy. Ever. Being without him as a separated parent had given me some freedoms, but it also significantly added to my lonely times. It's a conflict that every single parent feels, I'm sure.

On the non-custodial nights when my son was tucked up in bed at his mum's place, I got to enjoy the feeling of old freedoms, without the worries of stumbling barefoot onto sharp Lego pieces or being woken up at the crack of dawn and being asked to play Minecraft with a thumping hangover. Late nights of over-indulgence could be remedied with uninterrupted sleep-ins and when I couldn't be bothered making a cooked meal that ticked all the boxes of sensible nutrition, I'd simply make myself some eggs on toast or call in a delivery, if that's what I felt like doing.

But then there were the other times…

Those child-free moments when I wondered what he was doing, who he was talking to at that exact moment in time, what funny story from school I'd missed or how I wasn't around when he and my ex came up with some funny joke known only to them. Being a separated parent pining for my boy was a special level of loneliness, for me. It could start off as a little ache but could then morph into something that felt almost like a sort of amputation. It often felt as though a perfect part of me was missing and, although nobody could see it to notice exactly what kind of pain I was in, it scratched at me and tugged at my heart and made me feel like my blood was constantly seeping from some invisible wound. If I wasn't travelling, it wasn't too bad. If I was in a similar, non-sex work-related environment, I still felt a connection to him. But if I was on an overnight (or multi-night) booking internationally, interstate or even right near home, the pain was amplified and I simply had to block his beautiful little face from my thoughts in order to do my job. It was a constant struggle that took a long time to overcome.

But then, just as quickly, a night would arrive when my boy and I were back under the same roof and I'd be annoyed about him missing the toilet or pushing my buttons with his all-too-familiar attitude. If I wondered too long about exactly how long I could be a sex worker, I found myself laughing at the potential scenario of me, five years into the future, being invited into the classroom with all the other dads and mums, to talk to the kids about what I did for work.

'I try to help women remember that they can love themselves,' or

'I help mend broken hearts,' or simply,

'I fuck women.'

None of them look particularly good on paper and somehow, I don't think I'd make the cut of parents delivering presentations on career day.

Did it bother me? No. Not at that stage.

Did I think it would bother my son?

The idealistic part of me wanted to say 'no' because I wanted to raise him to be tolerant and accepting of differences. But I knew that might not be the case. The world is not that wonderful. I was proud of what I did, but I was also bound by a broader understanding of how other people's judgements could be constraining. Just like I hadn't yet told my parents what I did for a living, I couldn't possibly even begin to think about how I would discuss it with my son. I was his champion. I was the motorbike-riding cool dad who worked out, played Minecraft with him and had a body that looked better than most of the other dads he'd see at school pick-up. I knew that perception wouldn't last forever but while it was there, I was in no hurry to add any more confusing layers.

I went into escorting to find long-term work that I loved but how long I kept it from him, I guessed, would be up to him. The questions would eventually come, I knew. I once asked him what he thought I did for work and he simply said,

'I don't know. You make people feel happy, I guess.'

My heart almost burst when he said it, as it felt like he understood the true purpose of my job when many adults still didn't understand. In reality, though, I knew his were the words of a naïve young boy who was still self-absorbed and not interested in what his old man did for a living. It still felt wonderful, though. He obviously wasn't ready to ask anything yet, but when the time came that he was, I wondered, would I be ready to answer?

Chapter 25 – Catching The Feels

As far as second dates go, this was a fun one. It was an unusually chilly weeknight in Brisbane and instead of the usual dinner/hotel-type booking, this was more akin to a revenge date – except the target arsehole wasn't actually in attendance.

Anna had already sowed the seed by casually mentioning she had a new guy in her life to a couple of the mothers in her little group prior to that night and I was only too happy to play the part for her. I love pub trivia nights and, thanks to a slightly overzealous competitive streak, I'm often a great team-mate to have, because I love to win.

Admittedly, the idea of taking a paid male escort to a trivia night is unusual, but I could see that Anna really wanted to make an impression and by having me on her arm, it was almost certain that at least one of the parents at that gathering might report their sighting of us back to her former husband. Our strategy worked perfectly, too. I tried to make sure that I was the most charismatic, worldly guy in the room – the guy everyone wanted to talk to and, I secretly hoped, the guy that a couple of the other mums wanted to go home with.

We ended up in a team with two other couples. Playing the part of Anna's new boyfriend 'the photographer' became quite exhausting after we broke off into smaller groups for the actual competition. When I was asked about work that night, I couldn't simply say, 'I'd prefer not to talk about it', as I usually did when I didn't feel like outright lying to someone. Instead, I was forced to speak in-depth about the work I once did but speak of it in the present tense. That made it easier, but it was still unpleasant and it felt like a constant reminder to Anna that our relationship was temporary, and not the beginning of a loving partnership, as we'd led others to believe. There were a few particularly heavy moments when Anna's good friend told her how much she liked me and that I was a 'keeper' who clearly adored her. I did adore her of course, but I was definitely not someone you made long-term plans with.

On the way home as we held hands in the Uber, she rested her head on my shoulder and told me how grateful she was for the respect and affection I'd shown her in front of her friends. It saddened me that such a wonderful, kind and funny woman had to pay someone like me just to feel appreciated and a huge part of me was amazed she'd chosen me and allowed me into her life.

I often reflected on how my work introduced me to so many incredible women. The reasons they chose a male escort were complex and what they gained from the experience was just as multi-layered. But often, I was gaining a lot too, and in those special times, doing what I did felt like a gift.

Making love to her later was beautiful. The events of that evening made me feel as close to 'normal' as I had any time since being with my wife. So normal, in fact, that a small part of me felt guilty. I imagined that I really was in a proper relationship with a new person and quickly realised that I was far from ready. I knew I couldn't be with my ex anymore, but I also knew I couldn't be with anyone else, either – and I secretly hoped she felt the same way. That was only the second time that Anna and I had seen each other, but the way we explored each other's bodies felt strangely familiar, yet still exciting, all at once. It left me feeling excited for a future that would never be, so also very, very confused and a bit deflated.

Chapter 26 – Betrayed

Sam was with another escort?! She told me in a text – and it took quite a while to let it sink in. Soon afterwards, she added,

Don't worry, Dan, he was as dumb as dogshit.

Her unsympathetic assessment made me laugh but there was something else pushing against that feeling and it was clearly jealousy.

From a professional perspective, I worried for a moment that this long-term promise I thought we had, as escort and client, was already ending and I'm slightly ashamed to admit, my mind quickly crunched the numbers to imagine what the financial aspect might look like without Sam's regular bookings. The personal perspective overtook, though. I was invested. I didn't mean the hours I'd spent calling and texting her or reading about her prognosis, either. It was my soul that seemed to hurt.

I felt angry and betrayed, and wondered how could she cast me off like the whore I was, with so little regard for my feelings? Trying to remain as detached as possible, I realised I'd probably encouraged her by inviting her to ask me about any other male escorts she was considering. But that was a half-hearted offer, made only to ensure her safety. And I wasn't even consulted about this guy! She said he'd won one of those bullshit awards they give for escorting and therefore assumed he'd be okay, and that she didn't want to bother me. With my mental health on its usual shifting sands, deciding to be with Sam had left its mark on me already and the idea of her being with another escort sent a series of unwelcome images into my mind.

Would he walk her home to make sure she could get in safely?

Would he take advantage of her failing memory?

Would she tell him how much he mattered to her, as she told me?

Was he better in bed than me?

It was late when I found out and I knew I should've been getting ready to sleep, but I remembered a little stash of coke that I had left on a plate in my bedside table drawer. I decided to finish it. Fuck it. Fuck all of it. The bitterness dropped to the back of my throat and I doubled down by having a big nip of straight, icy-cold vodka to wash it away.

I told myself I felt better already, and told myself not to worry about Sam and that other guy. I thought I'd better text her back regardless of how I felt, as that would be the professional and caring thing to do, after all.

I hope everything was okay – and you had fun! I lied.

But she didn't reply. As the coke kicked in and my heart rate lifted, my feelings started to dissipate. I put some headphones on, turned on a few beats and poured another drink. *Sam would be back,* I thought. Surely, she'd be back.

Chapter 27 –
A Heavy Weekend in the Tropics

After our romantic weekend away in the Yarra Valley, Christy and I stayed in regular contact but only went on one more dinner date. When one of her two beloved horses died a couple of months later, though, we began to speak almost daily and hearing her tell me all about how she and her kids were coping reminded me of how much she had opened up to me since we first met – and her trust was something I was honoured to accept.

A few weeks after that, she invited me to go away with her for a few days to celebrate her fiftieth birthday – in tropical Port Douglas, this time. Once again, she was her usual doubtful self – constantly checking and double-checking to make sure I wanted to go, giving me plenty of opportunities to back out and generally questioning why I wanted to be with her. I probably didn't say it enough at the time, but I really loved her company. Her dry, sarcastic sense of humour perfectly matched mine, and she was great fun in bed – especially when she let herself go as she did when we were first together.

She took the plunge, eventually, and booked everything. A couple of weeks later, we were off. We stayed in a luxurious villa right on the main street and it was there that we shared a couple of very special moments that I'll never forget. On the second night, we'd drunk a fair bit over dinner at a restaurant within walking distance so, after stumbling back to our room, we decided to have a shower together for a bit of fun. It was one of those massive showers designed for two, so I thought I might improvise a bit by dragging one of the deck chairs from the pool, up a flight of stairs and into the shower so she could lie down under the warm water while I went down on her. It felt like she was my Cleopatra and I was her servant. I'll never forget looking up and seeing her in total bliss and loving every second. The whole experience was almost surreal.

It was at times like that when escorting offered all the fun and excitement of the early days of a relationship, but I still wasn't sure how far we should go. Christy was on a powerful journey and I felt honoured to have been chosen to walk some of it with her, but I was also conscious of how close we were becoming. I began to question whether such an attachment was healthy for either of us. The attachment only grew stronger on that trip, when the following night she revealed to me that she was petrified that she might have cervical cancer. She'd had some preliminary blood tests and it didn't look good. She hadn't told anyone else about it at that point – not even her kids – and my heart felt heavy when she shared the devastating news. Christy and Dan sobbed as a boyfriend and girlfriend would before Mitch stepped in to lighten the moment by focusing on the positives. I could tell that she was overwhelmed by a diagnosis that hadn't officially been made yet, so together, we researched what the likelihood was that she actually did have cancer. We also looked at what the survival rate was – as well as what the treatment would look like. It wasn't the sort of exercise one envisages when going on a romantic weekend away but by sharing her pain, I felt I was providing her with a service that was far more valuable than just sexual relief.

Christy was one of the most impressive and inspirational women I'd met through my work and, although I knew that we would stay in touch, I felt just as certain that, without me to hire as an escort, she would soon find herself in a different kind of self-discovery back in the real world. When we said our final goodbyes at the airport back in Melbourne, it was with a hug and a long kiss filled with all the tender memories we'd shared in that brief, intense time in each other's lives.

Our correspondence was scant after that weekend, but several weeks later, I saw a message pop up on my phone:

OMG Dan, I just had to tell someone – biopsy all clear! I am so bloody relieved!

I was the first person to hear the good news and, I suspect, the only person with whom she had shared her journey with in the first place. It was such a joy to have been a part of her life during that difficult time and I was so relieved for her. She'd put up with so many years of walking on eggshells and living in fear of her unpredictably violent husband, it was wonderful to see her finally catch a break now she'd left him and forged on alone as she entered her fifties.

We stayed in contact for a few more months after that and she shared various stories of awkward online dates with more sub-par men seeking emotionless sex. After a while, though, we drifted apart. I still often think about her and with all my heart, I wish her a lifetime of happiness.

She certainly deserves it, and I really hope she's found it.

Chapter 28 – My Three Serves

My new client told me she'd seen a couple of escorts before, but that was several years ago...

She explained that she was quite happy to pay each time because she figured a professional would be less judgemental and more open to her 'sexual preferences'. She didn't want a relationship either – she wanted to 'explore her sexuality' and didn't feel comfortable doing that with someone she was seeing on a more permanent basis. Normally, I'm a bit wary of clients who have been with a lot of escorts, and the vanilla part of me was concerned about these 'sexual preferences', but we'd spoken a couple of times already and I got the impression that she was very laid-back and quite cute.

My predictions turned out to be true. When she opened the door that night, I was greeted by an absolutely stunning, Middle Eastern lady somewhere in her early forties. Or so I guessed. It turned out that she was turning forty-nine in a matter of weeks, and that just ticked all the boxes for me. She had a sharp, well-defined face and incredibly dark (almost black) eyes, long, thick dark hair and a huge, welcoming smile. Over the years I've been fortunate to have been with women from all sorts of cultures. I enjoyed learning all about them and of course, I loved exploring their bodies. This particular client was Palestinian. Given I wasn't her first escort, the competitive side of me immediately wondered why she hadn't contacted me earlier but I quickly pushed the thought aside to stay in the moment and to focus on what was to come. She mentioned that she liked toys, and that sounded pretty fun to me too, actually. I was secretly looking forward to the focus being off my cock for once, as it'd let me down a couple of times recently and my confidence was suffering.

She'd just ended a long-term relationship that both she and her partner had tried to spice up by using escorts. The first time, they chose one each, saw them in separate rooms to start with and then all met together shortly afterwards for a foursome. My client said she hated it and that it wasn't long before the husband continued seeing escorts alone. I could tell that that still pained her, so I decided not to press her for any more details.

As we sipped on some Prosecco, she gave me a quick tour of her recently acquired, inner-city townhouse. It revealed all the usual trappings of a successful, professional woman, ready for a new life on her own. There were vases with fresh flowers, a few scented candles burning and quite a few old photos dotted around the place, showing her and her friends on globe-trotting adventures. I also noticed a doctorate hanging proudly in her little home office, which was another little turn-on to me.

She led a healthy lifestyle and the evidence was all around us, from the yoga mat rolled up against the wall to the resistance bands in the lounge room in front of the television and the kitchen bench filled with every possible appliance to juice and extract. Conversation flowed very easily between us, as there was clearly a strong mutual attraction, and before we knew it, we were kissing passionately on the soft rose-coloured sheets of her huge bed.

After roughly half an hour of gentle play, she excused herself to go to the bathroom and when I heard her open the refrigerator door followed by the beeps reminding her to close it, I assumed she was bringing back a drink, so I propped myself up, waiting.

When she walked back in, she was carrying a big Tupperware container and as she brought it closer, I could see that it contained a few fruits and vegetables.

'Are we having a picnic?' I smiled as I asked, still slightly unsure.

She laughed as she set the container down on the bedside table. 'Too much?'

I shrugged and just chuckled – I was once again totally out of my depth, but willing to give it a go – the story of my life.

To ease us both back into the mood, I straddled her, took off her underwear and reached for her body again. I was tracing my fingers around her breasts and brushing them lightly over her nipples when she took my hand and guided me over to the collection of fresh produce she'd put on her bedside table. She led me to the carrot first and I held onto it so I could run the top of it very softly along her belly and down between her thighs. She giggled and I felt her body twitch against the cold touch of it. After she laid down again, I gave the carrot a few puffs of my breath, like I was cleaning spectacles, in an attempt to warm it up a bit, but it didn't help much. I then tried putting a tiny bit of lube on it before slowly sliding it in. She was pretty wet already and so turned on that she kept pushing my hand with hers, forcing the carrot to go further and deeper inside her, until at one point, it was more than halfway in. If it hurt her at all, she gave no indication of it whatsoever. Her mouth reached up towards mine and we kissed for a while before she pulled the carrot out from between her legs and raised it seductively to my lips.

'Bite?'

Her voice was an incredibly sexy, cheeky whisper – made even more seductive with her slight accent. I didn't have much choice in the matter as she insistently pushed the carrot tip into my mouth.

Hmm... I thought. *This is new.*

As my teeth crunched into it, I tasted hints of her and it was great. My client's sweet bitterness combined with my favourite vegetable. It was sexy as all hell and I was a bit peckish too, which helped. Her eyes were bright and wide and she had the cutest little smirk on her face as she watched me. It was apparent that she really liked how much I was enjoying her little game.

The booking that night was a slightly longer one – five hours – so she obviously had a decent amount of disposable income and that little collection of fruit and veggies made me glad I hadn't had much for dinner that night. I really like carrots so I ate most of it before we moved on.

The next few hours were a whole lot of stress-free fun. In between sessions of kissing and cuddling, we went through a cucumber, a zucchini and even a strawberry, which she deliberately made a little bit squishy inside her warm skin for me to slowly nibble and lick out of her. I remember at one point I took a break to go to the toilet and when I got back to the bed, I found her looking curiously at the head of a small piece of broccoli. It was hilarious to both of us and fortunately, she put it back.

As we approached the three-hour mark, I felt like I'd eaten more than my daily recommended intake already, and to be honest, the whole food thing was getting pretty old at that point, so in an attempt to break things up, I asked if I could take a shower to re-energise. By the time I got out, her attention finally turned back to me and we had some pretty athletic and sweaty sex, with my own body filling hers as I held, kissed and stroked her to a wonderfully vocal orgasm. It was almost like I'd been starved of attention and that only made me hornier. Given that she had come, and because we had less than an hour to go at that point, I took this as licence to let myself go too and the constant edging all night made it an incredibly sharp and intense orgasm for me too. It was the sort of sex that left the sheets saturated and when she eventually got up from the bed to offer me a cold drink, I was very happy to accept. The softness of the pillow beneath my head reminded me how exhausted I suddenly felt but my eyelids had barely closed before the loud whizz of her blender roused me. I sat up in bed in time to see her return with a couple of glasses containing some sort of juice.

I subtly glanced at my watch, relieved that her time was almost up and thought, *Ugh. This is the last thing I need. Just give me a God damn vodka!*

Chapter 29 – The Gifts

Since the first time she booked me, my much older construction tycoon and I stayed in fairly regular contact. Because she was based in Perth and we couldn't see each other as regularly as she would've liked, she was happy to pay for video calls that she said helped remind her of what she was missing. Then, because she got sick of waiting, she booked me again – but this time for a whole weekend.

I insisted on paying for the flights that time because (a) I had enough points for business class, and (b) I could then make a tour out of it and promote it online to let people know that Mitch was heading west. Although my time with her would form the bulk of my weekend, I knew I'd have a few days afterwards for other clients and I was hoping to establish a bit more of a presence over there, while potentially seeing some clients I'd been flirting with during lockdown.

She seemed a bit annoyed when she found out I planned on taking other bookings after being with her but I assured her that her time with me was exclusive and nothing would come between us during our days and nights together. It was also a very subtle way of reminding her that this was my full-time business and not just a fun little frolic for me. She appeared to be okay with it eventually and seemed to understand where I was coming from.

'Well, I'm glad I'm first at least because I've got lots of plans for us.'

She said it to me with a chuckle and also told me about a present she'd bought for me – something she was going to give me when we met. It wouldn't be my first present but I was super grateful at the thought. One perk of being an escort is that some regular clients love to bestow gifts to remind you how special you are to them, and this client had already been very generous to me in the past.

I told her that I hoped she hadn't gone to too much trouble and I genuinely meant it. As flattering as it was to be on the receiving end of a new diamond ring, gold chain or expensive watch, there was an element of ownership that comes with the territory and when it came to this older client; I wasn't sure how healthy it would be for our relationship to continue too much longer. A thirty-year age gap was a big one for me and it required a mental shift to balance what I believed I should be giving to clients who wanted me and what I needed to be giving to myself in order to feel good about my choices.

It was a constant internal struggle that often made me feel superficial, so I pushed it away while telling myself it didn't matter and that I should be happy to have clients who were so willing to spend money on me and so willing to be generous. But when sex work makes you do things that you'd never normally do in real life, it raises the question about what parts of yourself you might be losing and what price the choices you make have on your self-esteem and pride.

On that occasion, my client surprised me with a pair of incredibly expensive but overly flamboyant Christian Louboutin sneakers that looked completely ridiculous and more suited to a teenager or rapper, but I was able to exchange them later. I was grateful and I have no doubt she had the best of intentions but, given the cost, I thought they should be something I would actually wear.

Had I become a person who would now do anything for money though? And if I had, what would I be capable of next?

Chapter 30 – Loyalties Tested

When Sam called to tell me some hard truths her specialist had delivered about her disease, I was one hundred per cent present to acknowledge and to listen, but she said she wanted to see me in person. She asked me to come visit her ASAP and wasn't coy about the fact that she also wanted to get 'a bit kinky'. In one sentence, she was telling me about the terrible realities of her diagnosis and how some upcoming genetic testing she was booked in for would soon reveal whether her kids may get the disease too. She sounded defeated for a heartbeat, but then the conversation suddenly flipped to sex and she started to tell me all about what she wanted me to do to her when I next saw her. How she wanted to be on top more and that she wanted me to come in her mouth this time. It was becoming too much. My brain had trouble keeping up with her mood fluctuations but I tried. If she could do it, then surely I could, right?

We made a booking for two days later. I started worrying about how to switch from listening to her fears about forgetting her children's names, to thinking about what positions might add some excitement to her sexual experience. I was providing a service, after all, so my worries expanded to stress around making sure she was satisfied as a client, along with my new concerns about her financial situation. When I first met her, I thought I was meeting a successful, professional woman with plenty of money to spend on her dying wish for sexual happiness, while she still had an appreciation for its pleasure. It didn't take long for me to realise, however, that divorce – and her ex-husband's fresh commitment to a new girlfriend and her kids – meant that he had his own financial pressures to consider and that Sam's money was not as freely accessible as I'd been led to believe. Money was becoming a regular conversation between us, and before she booked me, she now tended to check the price, then complain about it before asking for a discount. On one occasion she decided to cancel the booking when I wouldn't budge.

'Boyfriend experience' bookings became less expensive 'coffee date' bookings, with almost no notice given. We were talking almost daily via text or phone anyway, so asking her to hand over several hundred dollars just because I picked her up for coffee was becoming something I found difficult. The number of times I'd gone unpaid was growing but so was my attachment, and the friend who had initially reached out to me didn't seem to be in a hurry to add much clarity, either. I began to feel guilty about maintaining a business-like approach to ensure my services were valued, because Sam herself had so many other things to think about. It gnawed at me, relentlessly.

Did escorts work pro bono? If they did, then this surely would have qualified as worthwhile, but I had rent to pay and philanthropy was not what I signed up for. The relationship between the sex I was selling and Sam's desperate grasp on their former vibrancy was something I found difficult to process. It felt almost existential.

I psyched myself up for the booking she'd made and decided to worry about how I'd be paid afterwards. Sam needed me. Or at least, I thought she did. Then my phone beeped a message and it was her again. She said she couldn't make that booking and she wanted to change it to the following Friday instead. So, I wrote back.

Okay. Sure. I hope everything's alright.

But when I put the phone down, my frustration took over. Did she even value my time? I found myself getting angry at a dying woman and it felt like she was messing with my head and my business. I wondered, did she need me or not? As always, a little vodka helped dull my frustrations, but it didn't stop me from hating myself for questioning my motivations.

Chapter 31 – Assaulted

I'm a fairly vanilla kind of guy compared to most in the sex work world – I think I've established that. It's hard to believe, I suppose, when you consider my work and my use of chemical substances but, when it comes to sex, I like it fairly straight. Definitely no real pain. Not the kind to make you seriously hurt and leave scars, anyway.

The texts and emails kept coming, though. I mostly got enquiries from people who asked if I was the dominating type but occasionally, I'd get some from people who wanted to dominate *me*. I was asked about candle wax (sure, if it's the safe, low melting point type) and about bondage (soft ropes are okay, hard chains are not) and, on a couple of occasions, I was even asked about knife and needle play. I tended to just ignore those, though, because it's obvious they were just time-wasters who hadn't bothered to read my online ads.

So, when I turned up at the home of an early thirty-year-old and, after a few drinks to break the ice, she told me she wanted me to indulge her secret fantasy, I asked her what it was.

'Nothing too weird – I just want you to tie me up and hold me down while we fuck.' She was a fairly big girl with a strong, stout body, thick, muscly thighs and quite possibly the most enormous breasts I'd ever seen.

This'll test me, I thought.

Bondage was a slippery slope for me, and something she should've mentioned to me in our pre-booking phone call. I wondered how forced my smile looked, because I was definitely worried about where it was all heading. It was not sounding like me at all.

She took me to her bedroom and I saw the props she was hoping to use – some velvet cords for me to tie her up with and a satin blindfold. There was also a rubber gag, but I was damned if I'd be using that. This wasn't *Pulp Fiction*.

I honestly did get it, though. I respect women and never want to do anything to hurt them, but I do understand that, for some, a safe version of a power struggle could be a serious turn-on. It's just that I'm more of a bend-you-over-the-kitchen-bench sort of guy – and not much more.

We started to kiss and eventually undressed. I reached for the rope and wrapped it firmly around her wrists in front of her. I'm no Shibari master and can't hog-tie anyone to save my life, but I got there in the end with some very simple hitch knots I used when tying things down on my bike. I'd hardly ever done this sort of thing before but knew the importance of a traffic light system to let me know she was okay – but, I wasn't the least bit inclined to let it get even remotely close to that. I slipped the blindfold over her eyes and her smile told me she was satisfied. My body slid down hers and I kissed and stroked her gently in various sensitive places until my face arrived between her legs and my tongue reached out to her with long, smooth strokes against her skin.

Then, as I felt her body rise from the bed to press against my mouth, the pressure of her thighs squeezing around my head began to increase as she forced my head down with her bound-up hands. My mouth and nose were both well and truly muffled against her groin at that stage and she squeezed really hard while

I tried to subtly twist my body away. My head was locked into position, though. I was completely muffled and I was finding it virtually impossible to breathe. She had an incredible amount of strength in that area and the force quickly became really quite concerning. She began groaning and then growled at me.

'You fucking like that? Yeah?'

I was caught – literally – in the middle of someone's revenge fantasy. I felt a sharp sting against the back of my neck as she dug her long fingernails in, right near my carotid artery. With a force I really didn't want to use, and almost breaking my neck, I flipped her over and extracted my head from its position between her thighs.

'WHAT THE FUCK ARE YOU DOING!?' I was absolutely shocked.

She looked confused for a moment, then embarrassed. Then apologetic.

'I thought it would be okay. It was only my nails,' she muttered. 'You're okay, yeah?'

I sat up on the bed, didn't say a word, and untied her before reaching for my underwear.

'That wasn't cool at all,' I fumed. 'Ever heard of consent?!'

I walked into the ensuite and swivelled my head to loosen my neck and to assess the damage. I wasn't bleeding or anything but the scratches were clearly visible and it had scared the shit out of me. I muttered an apology, told her that it wasn't going to work and gave her an hour's worth of money back. She acted mortified and perhaps slightly angry, and I got an uneasy feeling she was also kind of enjoying it. It felt like she was proud to have dominated a straight 'alpha male' while also getting herself a discount in the process. To hell with that. I was done. Her request to kiss and make up was not where my head was at and I just wanted to get out of there – fast.

For some reason, I felt bad for letting her down, so I politely kissed her goodbye and told her I'd let myself out. At a 7-Eleven a few minutes later, I walked out with a Red Bull and a cup of their surprisingly good two-dollar coffee to clear my head before calling an Uber back home. The whole experience shook me up and reminded me to work on my communication. As I worked my way closer to St Kilda and my safe apartment, I made a mental note to more rigidly screen my new clients before I took any more bookings. Surprises are not my favourite things at the best of times, and when they came with sharp claws and thigh-holds, I liked them even less.

Back at home, I sent a message to my sex worker friend and told her the story. She sympathised with me, told me her own similar story and agreed it wasn't ideal. It also reminded me that the girls in the industry would feel even less safe in those situations, with many not simply able to get up and leave at the risk of escalating the situation further. I poured myself a drink and calmed down, and our chat soon turned into an invitation for her to come over and see me for some much-needed company. It wasn't the first time we'd spent the night together and although we didn't have sex, it was nice to have another naked body next to mine, without the expectation of performative pleasure. I think she needed to be held as much as I did, so that's what we did. We fell asleep eventually and woke up a few hours later, as the sun streamed in through the cracks in the blinds.

Another day, another dollar and yet another weird encounter.

I had a booking with a much loved, much more trustworthy regular the following night, so I drove my friend home on the way to a lazy session at the gym. When my phone beeped with a message, I saw that it was from last night's attacker – another apology for any misunderstanding and an invitation to try again – without the fingernails. She added that emoji with the goofy, tongue-out face that has one eye blinking and one eye wide open. I think it was supposed to be cute, but I interpreted it as crazy and just ignored her, and then blocked her for good measure.

I'd regained a bit of control and, even if I didn't end up with the money I was expecting, at least I walked away with some money in my pocket. I decided that the best way to deal with that near-trauma was to forget about it and treat myself to another bag of coke. I sent a quick message to my connection, hoping that I'd get it before my next job. It might not have been the best thing for my long-term mental health but in the short-term, it felt like exactly what I needed to work through the weirdness of my life. That's what I told myself, anyway.

And just like that, I was already feeling better.

Chapter 32 –
Doing The Daintree

It seemed I was on a roll. A bad one. Perhaps it was the drug use somehow tipping the forces of the universe against me or maybe I was just accepting too many dodgy bookings to make a buck, but whatever the case was – I was meeting some pretty average people.

Although I found that I could connect with almost every woman I met, some of them did test me – especially when their personalities turned out to be difficult. Kindness, humour and compassion are amazing traits in anyone and through my eyes, if a woman has those qualities, she already has the potential to be a gorgeous person, to me. But in the real world, the truth is, not every woman possesses supermodel-like characteristics – and not every person is a nice person. I was lucky that my encounters with women like that were few and far between but every now and then, if the stars weren't aligning for me, I'd get the double-whammy of a body type that did nothing for my libido, all wrapped around the personality of an arsehole.

That was what it was like when I met Phoebe.

Really, the initial phone call told me all I needed to know about her, but business had been tough during the pandemic and my bank account was busy playing catch-up. As a result, I think I'd become less discerning than usual – a corner that I'd promised myself never to cut again. One of JK Rowling's characters once said that if you want to get an idea of what someone is like, watch how they treat their inferiors, not their equals. Well, this woman was a prime example, but because I was too busy chasing a few dollars, I had committed myself and had to push on. Looking back now, it makes me cringe.

We met at an Italian restaurant in Fitzroy, so the travel time and lack of parking had me in a pretty shit mood to begin with – all for my bare minimum booking time of two hours. It was a nice enough place with an authentic old-school feel. There were pictures on the wall of various famous people, red and white checkered table cloths and the wonderful smell of pizza permeating throughout the place. The staff seemed really friendly and I felt myself finally beginning to relax. We hadn't said much at that point and I was looking forward to my first glass of chianti when I caught my first glimpse of the type of woman I was with. After putting on her small but thick reading glasses, she rolled her eyes and complained about the 'typical wog food' on the menu. I was stunned. Not only by the blatant racism, but also by her stupidity. We were sitting in an *Italian* restaurant! From there it only got worse. After ordering a steak and chips, she shot her hand up and barked out for a waiter to send her order back because it was too cold. I was totally embarrassed and wanted to get out of there and, surprise surprise, she walked out without leaving a tip – even though she had the poor staff constantly running back and forth from our table for the extremely long hour we were there.

She'd already been pretty cold to me on the phone, so by the time we walked back to her townhouse – just a couple of blocks away from the restaurant – I was having a hard time looking past her fairly rough appearance to find any genuine beauty hiding below the surface. As soon as we arrived back at her place – a typical two-storey townhouse sandwiched in between a few others – she walked straight upstairs to her bedroom. I reluctantly followed.

And then the time came to undress her.

At that stage in the proceedings, even if the person I was with didn't fit my perception of beauty, I could start to let my imagination run wild with the anticipation of the sights, sounds, smells and tastes that were about to be discovered. By then, my cock would normally have started to make himself known as I would run my hands along the body of the woman I was with, as I imagined my bare skin against hers – and it was usually enough to get me hard and ready. That night, though, with my mind still processing her bad attitude back at the restaurant and the silent walk back to her place, all I felt was worried. Gut-hugging underwear had been holding her in underneath her 50s-style dress, and when I peeled the garments away from her skin and I saw her soft, creamy flesh pour out from it like melted ricotta, I wondered if my grimace/smile was sustainable.

It wasn't her size as such, but more how hairy she was. There was absolutely no evidence of any sort of preparation for the booking as I took in the thick, dark forest before me. This was the time when I'd often sensually ask whether my client would like me to give her oral but, as my eyes took in the mounds of hair reaching from just below her belly button to a few inches down her legs, I stayed silent, as I wondered how I would even find my usual entry point.

Gravity and lube would have to be my guides.

Normally, I'd encourage my client to sit on the edge of the bed or couch and I'd kneel down and let my tongue and fingers do the rest. This time, I realised, if I sat her down like that, her body would completely cover the area I needed to access and, even if I could reach it, I'd have to burrow my way through the hair to reach it. As I imagined all this, I felt a complete absence of any sensation between my legs.

'Why don't you lie back and relax?' I offered.

I encouraged her to lay across the mattress, as close to the edge as possible and as her head hung back slightly towards the floor, I moved in, cupping the weight of her skin in my palms as I pushed upwards in the hope of being able to feel between her legs to get my bearings. It wasn't easy and the dimmed lights made it hard to visually confirm whether I was even in the right area. Unfortunately for me, it was anything but sexy but I closed my eyes and focused as hard as I could to see if I could get my usual meditation-style techniques to work their libido-enhancing magic.

The answer was a resounding 'no'.

I felt miserable as I knew it was going to be another one of those bookings where I couldn't get hard. I excused myself to go to the bathroom and grabbed my bag for some emergency Kamagra gel to toss down my throat. As its effects kicked in and my vision went pink (an irritating side effect), I just managed to get there, but it wasn't easy – and it certainly wasn't for long. The good things in life never are easy but then again, the same could be said for the bad.

That was another one of those bookings that I simply just had to erase from my memory. If I dwelled on it for too long, I'd find I started blaming myself and assuming it was all my fault. My competitive nature might also come out and I'd start to wonder if any of the other guys would have been able to pull it off – but I seriously doubted it. Even if they did, what difference did it make? I really needed to start going easier on myself and I needed to stop blaming my poor body when it didn't behave like the machine it was often expected to. Essentially, I needed to start chilling the fuck out.

Chapter 33 – Cathy

I've lost count of the number of women who have a history of sexual abuse or domestic violence, who decide to put their trust in a professional and book me. The first time I was told the story of someone's sexual assault, it shocked me and, in the setting of a booking, where I was expected to be sexy and sexual, it left me floundering. I wasn't sure how to react when faced with that initial outpouring of pain. In those early days, it felt like I was absorbing everything and I'd usually drive home with a very heavy heart. But the fact that ladies booked me for companionship, and more often than not for sex, as a way of furthering their healing, gave me a real sense of purpose and pride in the work I'd chosen to do.

Being allowed into someone's intimate space as their chosen sexual partner is incredibly meaningful and for the women who have had their self-esteem and choices taken away, the scars can be very deep. When the abuse begins in childhood at the hands of someone who should be caring for them, those scars are even harder to erase – but I don't believe it's impossible. I think that, given a lot of patience and time, and by acknowledging that you never did anything wrong in the first place, it's possible to move forward. I do also understand that for some women, though, it's a very hard thing to overcome and their feelings of self-hatred or worthlessness may never truly disappear.

I find it amazing that women who have had bad experiences with men even think of being with an escort, to be honest. Why would a woman who's had such a terrible experience with sex ultimately want to seek out sex with a stranger? After having it explained to me by the wonderful, brave women I have been with, I now believe I understand.

Firstly, it's down to sex itself, because sex can be bloody amazing. The truth is that, in the right setting, with the right person, it's a wonderful thing and the women who choose to see me want to be reminded of that. It's a significant part of the healing process to face a fear and then take control of it, too. By pushing past a barrier that may previously have made them not want to have sex ever again, they could be reminded that it didn't have to be a frightening thing – and, importantly, that they deserve the pleasure it brings.

The ones who spent far too many years being convinced that they were not worthy of genuine happiness were often the most difficult to convince. I could tell them a hundred times how attractive I found them or how beautiful I thought their bodies were, but I knew they didn't believe me. I could understand their scepticism given our transactional relationship, of course, but it still frustrated me at times, because I honestly was telling them the truth. Nevertheless, I kept telling them anyway and more importantly, I kept showing them. I'm transparent in almost all aspects of my life and this includes lovemaking. Despite how vulnerable it made me feel at times, I always showed my true colours with every single client, which could mean I might be grinning like an idiot when in the heat of passion one minute and then crying alongside them the next when sharing their pain. This left me feeling extremely vulnerable at times, but oh well – so be it.

I tried not to let it all get to me, though. I tried not to take the blame for other men because I knew it wasn't my fault either. But after reading news report after news report and seeing the damage that some men do to women, it can be hard to feel proud of being a man. Empathy can be an amazing thing but it can also be a curse, and my propensity to feel too deeply for too long became harder and harder to put on the backburner. But then again, perhaps that's all part of trying to be one of the good guys.

About a year or so after I entered the industry, I was contacted by a beautiful and very special client called Cathy. It seemed the whole city was feeling lonely and helpless as the pandemic took its hold so, as a way of generating some additional income, I offered 'virtual' dates, via video. It wasn't wildly popular but surprisingly, quite a few women reached out to me and Cathy was one of them. In that first 'booking', I clearly remember being stunned by her beauty as her image materialised on my screen. She had the kindest, most beautiful eyes, an incredibly sexy smile and a fabulous sense of humour and, being in her early thirties, was one of my younger clients at the time. After a bit of tension-easing banter, she explained to me that about five years prior, she had been the victim of a violent home invasion where she had also been sexually assaulted. She said she was currently in a relationship and had been for several years, but interestingly, she felt more comfortable telling me about her experience than she did her partner – so she hadn't told him yet.

We had a few of these 'virtual' dates and, as we got to know each other more, the banter turned more sexual and the clothes started to come off. It really was a weird world during lockdown. I'd never done anything remotely similar to phone sex before but as the months dragged on, it became the norm. After a while, though, restrictions were finally lifted and Cathy and I met in person. When I answered the door, I could see that she was even more beautiful than she'd appeared on screen, with flawless skin and beautiful hair as well as that incredibly sexy, cheeky smile. She was very shy though and very, very nervous. As was the case with my very first client, her words were no louder than a whisper and she could barely look me in the eyes. After a very long, very warm embrace, she eventually opened up though. We had an absolutely magical time that night, made all the more intense as a result of the sexual tension that had been building up between us over the previous few months of online chats.

I wanted Cathy to feel as comfortable as possible, so I tried to keep things light and carefree – I figured that if she felt like talking about what had happened to her, she would and if not, that was totally fine as well. We *did* talk about what had prompted her to contact me in the first place, and she explained that she wanted to get some sense of power and control back and that she wanted to feel loved not only by me but by herself as well. She was under no illusion that she was paying for that love but she understood how beneficial it would be for her to experience care and compassion, which I was more than happy to provide. We both knew that yes, money was involved, but we both knew that in the time that we were together and for the many subsequent bookings we had, the love we made was one hundred per cent genuine. When I told her that my care and affections for her were completely real, I knew that, deep down, she believed it – even though the voice of doubt kept whispering in her ear to try and convince her that she didn't deserve it.

It made me smile to hear her say that, when she booked me, she knew she didn't have to worry about me trying anything she wasn't comfortable with and that she was in a completely safe, nurturing space. We saw each other at least once a month after that night and each time it was different. Sometimes, we couldn't get enough of each other and the booking would start and end in the bedroom. At other times though, we might just kiss and cuddle for hours, and not have sex at all. The best thing about our relationship, though, was that we always had an unspoken ability to match each other's energy, so neither of us ever felt dejected or disappointed. I guess I strived for that with all of my clients, as that's the sort of connection that can lead to the truly mind-blowing, almost out-of-body-like sexual encounters.

Every booking with Cathy had moments that were fun, gentle, sexy and loving but, at some point – whether it was during foreplay or when were wrapped around each other in bed after making love for hours – she would lean into me and cry. Every single time. It felt like sex with me gave her the freedom to release every possible emotion. She knew I wouldn't judge her and, despite her constant apologies, she knew I didn't mind. I wished that every client I was with felt that comfortable but for some, sex was just sex and that notion of emotional depth was nowhere to be seen. It wasn't as rewarding for me but was still okay – and this is what being a 'provider' is all about. Providing whatever your client needs.

Cathy saw me regularly for years and I'm not afraid to admit that we loved each other dearly – and told each other as much. The journey we shared throughout all the lockdowns, the cold miserable winters and even during the rare summer months when life almost returned to normal was nothing short of life-changing for both of us. Being a companion who was part of someone's healing process, though, added an element that was almost sacred and in the hours after our bookings, whether I was either back at home alone in my apartment or immersed in the role of father to my beautiful little boy, the pain of her experiences tended to creep in and often rattled me. I could never remain truly detached – no matter how hard I tried – and it was in those moments (and particularly after a vodka or two) that tears would make my cheeks sticky as I sobbed for that amazing woman who trusted me and believed in me.

Chapter 34 – Confusion

My relationship with Sam was going from bad to worse.

Once again, Sam texted to say that my rate to see her the following Friday was too high – and then, barely half an hour later, she texted again to say she wanted to change that Friday's booking for the following Wednesday. I may as well have set up a template as an automatic reply:

Okay. Sure. I hope everything's okay.

The following day, I texted her to remind her of the booking and she wrote back to confirm, then wrote back shortly after to tell me that Wednesday had to be cancelled as well – she forgot her sister was coming to stay with her as support for when she received the results from the genetic testing she'd already told me about. She wanted Tuesday instead, but I was already booked. We settled on Monday. That way she could tell me all about the test results as well. But when that day came, she cancelled yet again as the test results were delayed and she was having a tough time coping with the suspense.

Okay. Sure. I hope everything's okay.

The results of the test came a day later and she called me as soon as she arrived back at her apartment after seeing her specialist. She was almost inconsolable. I could barely understand her as she sobbed into the phone. The news was that her children had an extremely high chance of suffering a similar fate to her and I had no words – so I said nothing. I had absolutely no way of consoling her and there was no positive spin that could be put on such devastating news but we did manage to arrange a catch-up so I could listen to her and hold her, and try to help in any way I could.

In the meantime, I tried to figure out how I was going to help myself when the time came.

Chapter 35 – Mitch The Whore

I was using a lot more coke. Way too much.

I knew that was bad, but I didn't care. I was barely stretching $2700 worth of it two weeks – and that was with a loyalty discount from my dealer, who had incidentally bought himself a nice new Mercedes C300. Half of which I'd probably paid for.

After many long nights of bingeing, it still somehow managed to surprise me how shit I would feel when I woke up in the afternoon having wasted yet another day. It was the guilt in my heart that hurt the most. Sometimes it felt like a dull, heavy weight; at other times it was a more intense, emotional pain that twisted through me like a blunt knife.

I wondered what having a panic attack felt like and researched what the symptoms were. My intention was to put my mind at ease but, invariably, it had the opposite effect, because the way my body felt matched everything I'd found online. My heart would sometimes go into short arrhythmias in the few moments after I woke up. I became genuinely concerned that they might escalate into a full-blown heart attack. But then, as usual, a couple of drug-free days would pass and things seemed to return to normal. I'd feel great. I'd go back to the gym to put my heart under a different kind of stress, convincing myself that I was a picture of health and a man who treated his body like a temple.

It usually took me around two days of chomping on kale and salmon for me to become bored again, so I'd make that familiar call to Mr Mercedes to help take me away from the mundane realities of life.

Despite the extra coke I was having, I was still pretty good about not using it at work. Turning up on a client's doorstep fresh from snorting a few lines was never going to end well and I'd learned that the hard way – or should I say the 'soft' way? – I was on to a good thing, and I was determined not to let drugs or booze ruin that for me. I learned very quickly the importance of staying away from anything that could minimise the strength of my erection and the reality was with coke, no matter how much it amplified my sexual thoughts and desires and kept me alert and attentive, it often turned the volume down on my ability to stay in optimal lovemaking condition. I found that if I had too much, I would become easily distracted not only during conversation but also during sex – and that risked severing that all-important mental connection I relied on. And when clients were paying for my time, that didn't do anybody any favours.

Admittedly, there was the occasional time when I did manage to pull it off. I'll never forget one truly bizarre booking I agreed to after a long afternoon of solo pity-partying when I was running low on money but sky-high on confidence. She was a first-timer but she came complete with a particular kind of arrogance that made her incredibly demanding. To her, I was the hired help and because she hadn't had sex in a very, very long time, she wanted lots of it and she wanted it for every single minute of the booking. For a guy like me, who doesn't turn on and off like a tap and has to genuinely put my heart in it to feel the moment, I love to start my bookings more gently. Flirting. Conversation. Gentle touch to tease the desire out of each other. But this woman wanted my cock laid bare the second I walked in the door and for the entire three hours, she treated me like a freshly-charged vibrator that needed to perform at top speed. She was fit and athletic – I'll give her that. But the stench of cigarettes that was embedded in her greasy, stringy hair, not to mention on her breath, combined with the eighties style 'snap' tracksuit pants she wore made me wonder when she was going to bust out a pipe and get on the meth. I'll never forget one moment after I suggested that perhaps it might be nice to have a quick cuddle on the bed to get in the mood again, how she sensually and seductively took a drag from her filthy homemade bong before declaring:

'I didn't pay for *hugs,* babe, I paid for *dick.*'

Even if the physical attraction was there, which it most definitely wasn't, I doubt I could've got myself up to pace again and in a home that was ripe with the scent of mould and cigarette smoke, my libido wasn't exactly on fire. After all, if she couldn't keep her house tidy, I wondered how long it had been since she'd changed her sheets. Worrying about her personal hygiene just added to my angst.

Having forsaken anything remotely considered 'loving' and, after peeling her hands away from my arse halfway down the hallway on the way to the bedroom, I tried to turn my annoyance into sexy banter by telling her how hot it would be if we could have a shower together. It worked. I managed to subtly avoid her roaming hands until she led me to the bathroom, where I almost started to regret my decision. I felt like I might actually get dirtier just from being in there with all the empty tubes of medications and skin care products on the floor, a dead plant on the window sill and a laundry basket overflowing with dirty clothes just next to the dirty and stained old, pink toilet. On the positive side, the soap scum on the shower screen made things a bit harder to see once we were in there.

I turned the water up as hot as I could stand it, in a desperate quest for some cleansing sterilisation. After one look at some pubic hair stuck in the sad remnant of a soap cake, I let her hold onto it and placed my hand over hers and helped her wash the suds over every centimetre of her skin. And because I was in no hurry to return to the bedroom, I decided to start it off right there in that tiny shower, using my fingers between her legs to get her excited before lying awkwardly halfway in and halfway out of the shower so she could ride me. She seemed keen to focus on my pleasure after a while, so I stood up and leaned back as she turned around and knelt between my legs. Her mouth on me was surprisingly nice, despite the occasional intrusion of teeth.

If you close your eyes and concentrate, you can pretend anyone is giving you a blow job. But the second I opened them and took in the junk everywhere and the worn 1980s carpet in the hallway (the door was open of course), I knew I'd lose it, so I focused on the steady rhythm and the sensation, and everything somehow managed to become okay. Strangely enough, as soon as I surrendered to the whole situation, I got quite into it. I began to feel like a dirty whore in a filthy dump of a house being sucked off by some random, and I bloody loved it. I think I literally giggled when I realised that's exactly what I was.

Her mouth was full of me when I reached one hand to her shoulder and the other to the back of her head as a signal for her not to stop. I remember thinking to myself, *ah fuck it*, as I let go and exploded inside her mouth. Afterwards, I helped her up and, after a quick kiss, she cupped the palm of my hand between her legs and whispered in my ear.

'I want to squirt in your mouth.'

I died inside as her husky smoker's voice brought me back to reality. She climbed out of the shower cubicle, grabbed a soggy-looking towel probably bought in the nineties and wrapped it around herself while beckoning me to follow. I didn't want to but with two hours and fifteen minutes of the booking still left, I didn't have much choice but to ride it out. For a guy who chose sex work to experience freedom, it was a reminder that freedom was something that always had to be fought for and on that occasion, I lost big time.

I think I got out of there with fifteen minutes to spare, thanks to her becoming so high that she started nodding off. The second I got into my car on that freezing cold night, I slammed it into drive and immediately left all memories of that job behind. I was amazed that once again I'd managed to pull it off, but this time there would be no polite 'thank you' texts and absolutely no chance of a future booking.

When I arrived back at home, I remembered I had a bit of coke left and, as I rummaged through the drawer to feel for the bag, I told myself that I'd only have a couple of lines. I knew I'd probably regret it, but I'd worked my arse off that night and couldn't care less. It was my Mitch version of self-care. As the spark of it sped up my heart rate, I looked for my phone and messaged my friend to see what she was up to. Less than half an hour later, she pulled up in an Uber, eager to share some more of my coke while watching me drain my vodka dry.

Sex work might've killed my interest in less interesting conversations about Netflix or petrol prices, but it gave the two of us lots of tales to compare notes about. As the music played and I wondered if it was too loud for my neighbours, we kept telling ourselves it was just going to be a quiet night and, at the time, I honestly think we meant it.

Chapter 36 – The Housemate

Professional single women were my biggest market which made sense because,

(1) they had the disposable income required to pay for my services, and

(2) they had the freedom to do what they wanted, with whomever they wanted – anytime they wanted.

The voice at the end of the phone told me she was a time-poor, emotionally independent but very senior accountant. She mentioned the name of the firm she worked for, so I responded with what I thought were some appropriately impressed comments. She was very friendly but I got the impression she was still coming to terms with what she was doing so it felt like she needed to justify her decision to me, or more likely, to herself. I heard that kind of talk a lot, actually. There shouldn't be a stigma around sex work but, of course, there is and it made sense that the first-timers would find it the most difficult to justify what they were considering doing. Admittedly, that's slowly changing, and the odd confessional you might read about in women's magazines where high-flying women admit to hiring escorts might help that slightly, but there's still a very long way to go. Given that I was actually *in* the business, I obviously found the whole arrangement quite normal and often forgot how it could be perceived. On more than one occasion I found myself on the receiving end of some pretty awkward silences when I misjudged my audience but there were other times when it was quite fun to shut down some boring humble-bragging corporate guy with a casual mention of what I did for a crust.

Hardly anything trumps being paid to have sex when you're a guy.

Anyway, the lady I was about to see had made her mind up, irrespective of how conflicted she might've felt. She would've liked an overnight booking but it wasn't right for her, she said. She told me she had a flatmate that would be out for the evening at a specific time, on a specific date, so she wanted to book me for three hours in order to try an escort for the very first time. She quizzed me on my fees in a way that I expected an accountant might, but she also seemed to understand my value and didn't quibble. I think she would've been hard-pressed to claim me as a deduction, somehow. When she gave me the address, she repeated it twice and mentioned the booking time again, carefully, as if she was speaking to someone who might not understand English. I repeated it back to her and reassured her I was locking it into my calendar.

Seven pm – this Thursday – three hours.

We said goodbye and I waited about half an hour before I sent my usual new client follow-up message, just to heighten the anticipation.

Thanks for the chat – I can't wait to meet you!

She replied with the date and time again – and then, as if adding an afterthought to what she must have realised was a very unsexy reply, she sent a second text.

I can't wait either.

Thursday arrived and my usual pre-booking routine unfolded.

I was still looking okay from my wax a couple of weeks prior and my morning workout had me feeling pumped. I quickly munched a mint as I buzzed the intercom at the entrance to her townhouse. It wasn't quite as I'd expected it to be. For an accountant like her, who sounded ambitious, career-driven and money-smart, I anticipated a more contemporary development with a fresher feel. The 1990s-era building looked nice enough, though, in its leafy setting, near a slightly daggy suburban shopping strip in the outer eastern suburbs of Melbourne.

She came to the door and was immediately recognisable from the photo she'd sent me – a neat dark brown bob, with perfectly tweezed eyebrows and a slightly shy smile. She seemed a bit flustered, though.

'You're a little bit early.' I was told.

I apologised and told her that traffic was lighter than I imagined. She had a quick glance into the street behind me and then finally ushered me in. I tried not to let her obvious nerves rub off on me, so I focused on what I always ask myself as I go into a booking with a new client:

What would Mitch do?

I slipped the palm of my hand across the small of her back and gave her my best attempt at a soothing, sexy smile.

'Please don't be too nervous,' I said. 'There's no rush.'

She smiled and the rosy glow of a blush spread across her cheeks.

'It's the first time I've done anything like this,' she told me. 'And my housemate is only out for a few hours.'

I nodded and kissed her hand as I took in the family photos she had dotted around the place and the old-school, massive sideboard that took up half of one wall – complete with glasses of various shapes and sizes.

'Any chance of a drink?'

When I asked if she minded putting some music on, she walked me past a cool old record player and vinyl collection in her living room and opened up her laptop to put on some Jeff Buckley. He was never my favourite but I could tell by how many of his songs she had loaded into her playlist that he was probably hers, so I hoped it would get her more in the mood. She went to the fridge and squirted some white wine from a cask that looked like it had been there for years, so I took a sip and then placed the glass on the table. Looking a little miffed, she jumped up and quickly grabbed a little doily thing and slipped it underneath.

'Sorry,' she said. 'It's just that that's the *good* table.'

I probably stared at the dark pine finish for a moment too long and then reached over to massage the back of her neck. I really liked her. She was awkward, cute and super quirky. When I asked permission to kiss her for the first time, she replied by leaning her face towards mine as our lips met.

I liked to linger on that part – especially when I sensed that a first-time client might've been nervous and wanted to go slow. I found her kissing was more urgent than I expected though and within just a few minutes, she grabbed my hand and asked if I was okay with us moving to the bedroom. It was a little bit quick for me but I went along with it anyway. When we got there, I noticed that it was much smaller than I thought it might be. It was tiny, really – and her double bed took up so much of the space that I barely took two steps into the room before my shin hit the bed's base.

Smooth moves, Mitch, I thought.

'Sorry,' she said. 'It's tiny, I know. My flatmate was here first, so I got the second bedroom.'

I had a loose order of events mapped out that, based on past experience, filled the right amount of booking time and allowed us to go at just the right pace. She seemed to be in a hurry, though, and as my lips traced their way across her clothing and my hands reached up to unbutton her blouse, she pushed me down on the bed and reached her own hands up to take over.

'It's okay. I've got it...'

She must've been hornier than I thought. As she lowered her now-naked body against the bed, her hands tugged at my wrists and she pulled me down to lie next to her. Our skin was a tangle of knees and elbows until we shifted around to find our space against each other on the small bed. We were on our sides, looking into each other's eyes and, as I leaned in to kiss her tenderly, I felt her hand behind my head, pulling me closer until our mouths met. I still wasn't that comfortable with how fast she was going but she was super-cute in that sexy librarian sort of way, so I let it slide. Foreplay was a rush of tongues and fingers before she shimmied backwards across the bed, with her legs spread wide around my back as she pulled me deeper into her. As our bodies moved against each other, we found our rhythm and we moved together – slowly at first, then faster and faster. I felt a surge and a rising heat that radiated upwards through my belly and chest.

I groaned quite loudly. As I liked to do.

'Ssssh!'

Her hand playfully covered my mouth but then pulled away just as quickly.

'Ooh, sorry!' I said.

I seriously doubted the neighbours could hear but, whatever. We eventually became more comfortable with each other's needs and began to make love in a manner I was far more used to. We'd been playing, then resting, then playing again and having a great time for an hour or so before all of a sudden, she abruptly rolled away from me and accidentally bonked her head on the wall.

'Did you hear that?!' she hissed.

If she meant the loud thump of a skull on plasterboard, I definitely did, but she appeared completely oblivious to what had happened. As I was about to question her further, I noticed her head was cocked to one side and one finger was covering her lips, while the other was pointed towards the front door. The jingle of a key in the lock was obvious now and her eyes widened.

'Oh, fuck!' She looked really panicked.

'Get your clothes on! Mum wasn't meant to be home for another hour and a half! Oh, fuck!'

What could I do? I didn't care less if her mother/housemate busted us. I didn't know either of these people from a bar of soap, so I tried to remain calm. Truth be known, I was struggling to hide my amusement at the whole situation. I didn't want to appear to be a complete prick, though, so I quickly swivelled off the bed and jammed my undies and t-shirt on. I was just in the nick of time. Without warning, the bedroom door crept halfway open and a baby boomer with a helmet-head hairstyle and large red glasses poked her head in.

'Oh, I'm sorry, darling!' And then to me, 'Oh, hello there!'

What could I say to a sixty-something-year-old woman who'd just come home from an evening out and then had the shock of finding a half-naked man in her daughter's bed? As I opened my mouth to speak, helmet-head withdrew from the doorway and all I could hear was her voice.

'I was just popping in to ask how your night was – oh and Jacquie said hi!'

I didn't know what to do, but with her mother barely metres away, on the other side of the door, the polite teenage boy inside me took over.

'Oh, hi there! My name's Mitch... Sorry – I'll be out of your hair in just a sec... um... lovely to meet you!'

I was so glad that I always took payment from new clients upfront; otherwise, that could've seriously hampered my efforts to make a hasty withdrawal. Her mother stood in the hallway for a little too long, apparently just as awkward as the rest of us. Then, as I pulled my pants up and sat down on the bed to reach for my shoes, I could hear her footsteps retreat down the hallway. I took the initiative to close the door completely. At that stage, my adorable client was hidden under the sheets with her face buried into one of her pillows and I'm not sure if she was more embarrassed at the idea of her mum catching her with me or the fact that her persona of an independent successful corporate woman had been dented by the reality that she still slept in her childhood bedroom in her mother's house. None of it bothered me in the slightest, so to lighten the mood, I gave her a playful little tickle to remind her that, really, it could have been much worse. When she eventually emerged from her hiding spot, I was relieved to see she was smiling, so I leant down to give her a peck on the cheek, thanked her again and suggested that next time, we should probably consider grabbing a room somewhere. But both of us knew only too well that there wouldn't be another time.

Chapter 37 – Attempting to Heal

Amy Winehouse knew what she was talking about when she said she didn't want to go to rehab but then again, precisely no one else in the history of the world ever wanted to, either.

I wasn't looking forward to the idea but I was beginning to think it was the right thing to do. I'd done it twice before and there was nothing fun or amusing about it. It's nothing like it appears in the movies. In the Hollywood version, there's always a slightly caustic yet endearingly zany character, who's simply trying to make sense of a crazy world while still managing to be incredibly funny and painfully insightful in between dark moments of despair. And when this person meets the other equally troubled and misunderstood inpatient, whose feisty attitude hides their heart of gold, love always blossoms. If kicking my bad habits really could be achieved in combination with some rollicking adventures, emotional epiphanies and the chance to walk hand-in-hand with someone towards a happier future, I'd almost be happy to sign up. But that was bullshit. The truth is, it's lonely, it's boring and it's nowhere near as fun as taking drugs and drinking booze.

Things had escalated quickly and I was going through at least a bag (a gram) of coke a day – starting with my breakfast coffee. I'd try to remain somewhat in control by restricting my drinking to

154

after 2 pm, but I could recognise that it was becoming less about having fun and more about just following a daily ritual. I was tearing through the money I'd worked so hard for and I knew it was time to stop. So, I did the adult thing and made the necessary calls. But while I waited for the admissions nurse to call back, I made sure to get myself in a chatty mood by polishing off a few more lines.

I'd been particularly morose and lonely for a long time and the continual, never-fucking-ending COVID lockdowns hadn't helped. When you're intimate with a few different women a week and constantly calling and messaging your most valued clients in your downtime, imagine how you'd feel if there were no clients to touch and kiss and care for. Yes, I know how incredibly privileged that sounds, but it really was a huge change for me. I wondered how much attention would ever be too much – or close to enough – for me, and with isolation making physical touch such a rare pleasure, I'd been wondering it even more. At home, with only my regular clients to keep chatting to, and the occasional 'Virtual Mitch' session bringing a few bucks my way, I was feeling even more emotionally volatile and even self-medicating hadn't helped in the ways I needed it to. My last trips to 'hospital' had been depressingly free of any characters who could be remotely described as zany and the truth was, rehab hadn't helped me completely rid myself of my demons for any significant length of time anyway.

The worst part for me, though, was the lack of privacy. In rehab, everyone knows your business. You don't even get the chance to cry alone at night in peace before someone shines a torch in your face, checking to see whether you've topped yourself. And sure, when you're in a building with thirty other drug addicts, you can always get yourself whatever you want, but it's at the huge risk that if you get caught, you're out and back to where you started – minus several thousand in hospital fees – and there's no fun in any of that.

Not only does everyone in there hear everything about you in the daily group sessions, but all the people you leave in the regular world find out your secrets, too. Going to rehab is hard to keep to yourself. In my case, it would be completely impossible. First, there's my parents. Working my way up to break the news about my career was hard enough without having to confess to a coke habit on top of what they already knew about my issues with alcohol. Then there was my wife – and, legally, she still was my wife – and the way my treatment would leave her without a second set of parental hands to help – and I did firmly believe they could still help. I *had* to believe.

My son was way too young to understand a lot of things and explaining why Daddy had to go away to the hospital despite not looking sick would be tough. I could've told him that I'd checked in to have a rest and a few check-ups but, even with his limited experience of what going into hospital meant, I think that would've freaked him out and made my precious little man worry that I really *was* sick. It was one more thing in an increasingly long list of things I needed to address with key people in my life and the main person I needed to be honest with, I guess, was myself. Meanwhile, I kept just waiting for that call back from the hospital...

Chapter 38 – The Results

How do you cope with the news that an illness you know is destroying you will also be passed on to your children? I thought of my own boy and I couldn't imagine. Sam seemed amazing about it, but I wasn't sure how much was her strength of spirit and how much was the illness's hold on her, and how it had diminished her ability to feel the full weight of raw emotion. Spending a sizeable chunk of our next booking talking about her genetic test results was heavy, and spending the remaining part of the booking talking about making videos of each other having sex was just as intense. In her more lucid moments and in the earliest days of her diagnosis, she told me how much fear she had that the faulty genes ruining her own life would have the same impact on her children. Forever the optimist, I always tried to keep her positive and honestly believed it was unlikely. But now it was coming true, and so was that research I'd been reading up about online. Her sexual appetite waxed and waned between rampant voraciousness and an almost apathy. The evening she received her results, she could barely be satisfied. At first, she grumpily chastised me for forgetting to bend her over to take her from behind as soon as we walked into her apartment, but then she went straight into talking about making videos to help remind her of who she was – and who I was.

The rollercoaster I was being made to ride with her – with its constant twists and turns – was making me terribly confused. I wasn't sure what I was expected to give back to her in the form of an empathetic ear to listen or the sexy whispers she needed to hear. But then, I also appreciated that what I was going through was absolutely nothing compared to her own pain. My heart ached for the woman she was and her unwanted devolution. If the small part I could play was to hold her hand, or stroke her hair, or listen to her sadness, or bring her to orgasm, I shouldn't complain. And so, I didn't.

And then, when I got home again, there were always other ways to take my mind of things.

Chapter 39 — Pain And Passion

It'd been a while since my last booking with Anna. In between, we'd managed to keep the mood alive through hot texts and the occasional late-night drunken phone call. And so, when she texted wanting to make a daytime booking for three hours when I was next up north, my excitement grew and the thought of being able to taste her, touch her and talk with her got me all hot and bothered and needing some serious private time. I used up some frequent flyer points and booked everything the following day. Fortunately, a couple of other ladies were also interested in seeing me too. There was something special about Anna, though. I'd really missed her.

When I arrived, it was an uncharacteristically rainy day, so we didn't bother wasting time meeting for a drink. The hunger we had for each other was mutual and when she suggested I come straight to her place, I immediately agreed. I was so ready for her I remember I got hard in the Uber on the way over there. It was like my body was magnetised or something.

I'd barely knocked on the door when she answered wearing only undies and a silk robe and, as she reached out for my hand to pull me into the hallway, my mouth found hers and I felt the immediate pressure of my groin against her as I pushed her back against the wall. We started kissing and our hands moved across each other's bodies as we played with each other. When it all became too much, I scooped her up and carried her to the kitchen and practically growled as I spun her around, ripped my pants down around my ankles, bent her over and took her.

Three hours quickly turned into five as we continually changed positions (and locations) and discovered new ways to please each other. She loved receiving oral as much as I loved giving it, and during our sessions of lovemaking, I couldn't seem to get enough of the her taste – and the way her body reacted to my touch. We finished by climbing into her huge shower together, where we held each other as the soap cleansed our sweaty skin. At the door on the way out, it felt like neither of us wanted to break free from the hug we shared as I gave her one last long and passionate kiss to say goodbye.

It took me a couple of months to come to terms with the fact that the goodbye that day really was goodbye. We continued to talk and text on and off for a while as she navigated the details of financially separating from her husband, whilst also beginning a relationship with a very fortunate new man. I never saw her again. Given the intense feelings we had for one another and the impossible situation we were both in, it seemed like the best possible outcome. The only outcome. Did she feel what I was starting to feel? Did she also share my faint, distant hope that our relationship could have the potential to turn into something real? I'll never know for sure, but I'm very grateful for the time we did spend together. I hope she continues to flourish on her own and I sincerely hope that she finally meets that guitar-playing cowboy she always dreamed of, who'd come galloping over the horizon to treat her in the manner she always deserved.

I felt so lucky to encounter so many fantastic women who had such unique ways of making me feel alive and appreciated. But for me, sadly, none of them could be forever.

Chapter 40 — The Elite

A trip to Naples to stay on a luxury yacht for New Year's Eve? Don't mind if I do!

It was back in December 2019, I'd been working flat out for most of the year and we'd yet to have our worlds turned upside down by the pandemic. I'd seen my new client Danielle a couple of times already at her place in Brisbane at that stage and we always had a fabulous time together. The sex was passionate and fun, and she always seemed to have an upbeat, positive energy that was wonderful to be a part of. One night, as I sat in a hotel room in Sydney, we exchanged a few texts before she just came out with it.

Hey, do you want to come to Italy with me for New Year's?

Danielle's approach to life was to grasp all opportunities and live for the moment. She was one of those rare people who genuinely seemed to walk her talk. I always sensed that she had money and I knew that she did most of her work overseas, but I never thought I'd ever be one of *those* escorts who travelled internationally. When I first put together my marketing materials to showcase Mitch to the world of potential clients, I'd never dreamed these kinds of opportunities could possibly exist. Yet there it was.

To my estranged, yet incredibly supportive and loving ex wife, it was a sign that perhaps there really was no turning back from this. I was making this escort thing work and I was about to jet off to the other side of the world (first-class, mind you) with a woman who had money to pay for my time, as well as any expenses to cover my accommodation, dining and leisure.

From an hourly rate perspective, it wasn't going to be incredibly lucrative, but it was somewhere else that wasn't here. It was an escape and a once-in-a-lifetime experience. It meant being away from home for two weeks and that meant being away from my son, and I knew that my sadness would be difficult to hide. But work was work, so I tried to put that thought out of my mind so I could get on with planning.

Prior to the trip, my waxing and workout routine had ramped up a few notches in preparation and I spent a whirlwind week dashing from one appointment to another, in between shopping and packing as lightly as I could with a whole cross-section of outfits that ranged from casual daywear for general touristy stuff, business suits to allow me to mingle with her work colleagues and even my tuxedo for the New Year's Eve celebrations on the magnificent seventy-foot yacht she co-owned with her business partners. Shirts, jackets, sneakers, dress shoes... I made sure I covered all possibilities and even managed to tuck a few of my favourite sex toys and restraints into the suitcase. I thought of my bags going through x-ray and was grateful they weren't in carry-on.

Overnight bookings are an exhausting part of my repertoire because they come with all the added complications about how you sleep next to this other person, which side of the bed is whose, what time you both go to sleep and wake up, and so on. I was feeling an added level of nerves about this trip because it meant multiple days and nights with someone I didn't know particularly well – and on the other side of the world, far from any safety net of friends, family and familiar spaces and places. Danielle was incredible, though, so I needn't have worried. She understood the financial reality that she was scoring my time for a heavily reduced rate, in exchange for an unforgettable experience of insane luxury. With that understanding came her willingness to leave me to go and do my own thing sometimes, while she tended to some specific things she had no need for me to hang around for, so I had a bit of freedom as well.

The New Year's Eve celebrations kicked off in the morning as we departed the marina in the company of around ten of her closest uber-wealthy friends. We spent the day sunbaking, drinking and laughing a lot before everyone got dressed up for dinner. Danielle looked practically regal with her long, dark hair fashioned into a bun that accentuated the pearl necklace she wore, which was complemented by a pair of huge diamond earrings. The long, dark flowing dress with its plunging neckline and black stiletto shoes completed her flawless look. After we'd all rung in the new year (and what a year it turned out to be), Danielle and I found ourselves curled up in a suitably magnificent cabin, surrounded by scented candles with chilled downtempo music playing quietly in the background. In the early hours of that morning and while we were still a little bit drunk, we experimented with sensory play using the soft ties and blindfolds, which, when combined with the gentle rocking of the yacht, created a magical, almost surreal experience. Making love on a yacht was a wonderful new experience for me and the gentle sway produced by the sea made it all the more sensual.

Away from the bedroom, we acted like tourists, laughed constantly and enjoyed each other's humour – especially after a few glasses of very fine wine. I wished Mum and Dad could see me (well, not everything), so they could acknowledge that my lifestyle as a male escort was not always seedy and overly sexualised. Most of the time, sex work was about being a provider of support and companionship and for me and Danielle, it was definitely reciprocal.

By the time we left Naples, we were regularly immersed in deep discussion about our relationship and we talked openly about how valuable we were to each other, and how we had moved beyond the simple provider/client relationship to establish what seemed to be a permanent, paid lover scenario. For Danielle, the benefits of that relationship were obvious and appreciated. She made great money and had disposable income, so by paying for my services, she was protecting both her financial and emotional interests with a guy she knew wasn't going to betray her and someone who wasn't interested in controlling her by putting restrictions on her freedom. There was no danger of me putting in a de facto claim against her superannuation or her business and, of course, I knew her body intimately and understood what she liked to do to achieve maximum pleasure. If you could afford it, who wouldn't want that?

It was a fairly intense couple of weeks and after a couple of nights in Rome, it was time for me to head back to Melbourne. She asked if could stay longer, but the pull of seeing my son again proved stronger than the incredible feeling of being immersed in the fairytale I'd been so lucky to experience. Our emotions, despite our attempt to maintain professional boundaries, spilled over into a really difficult couple of hours at the airport, with both of us sobbing and finding it hard to say goodbye. I was grateful that her friend eventually arrived to drive her from the airport. I felt reassured that Danielle had someone to support her emotionally and to be some company for her on the drive back to her hotel. I couldn't help but be flattered by her love; despite my strong feelings for her, I worried that we might be on the path of becoming too close and that her whole speech about our ideal modern relationship, with her wanting to pay my way in and out of her life when she needed me, was more dream than reality. It can be hard to let go of old ways. So many of us see our parents divorce or we go through our own relationship break-ups so we naturally become cynical and want to find a better way to love and live. Some of us attain it, while for others, it's more of an endless search for fulfilment and connection, and because the old rules are so entrenched and expected, we find it hard to live the way we know we should, no matter how willing we are to try.

After a long and heartfelt embrace, I wiped away Danielle's tears along with my own, thanked her for my amazing Italian adventure and lifted the back of her hand to my lips as a final, romantic kiss goodbye.

Once I arrvied back in freezing cold Melbourne, I saw the marks of Danielle's mascara and tears on my t-shirt and the whole trip felt like a dream. I had school holidays to slide into and it was time for me to step up and look after my son. I was also extremely grateful that, from a financial perspective, I was now able to stay afloat whilst I took that short break to be with him.

Europe was fun, but an extremely rare opportunity. I couldn't count on jobs like that to keep paying the bills and I had my other beautiful clients back home asking to see me. It was time to get serious again and I needed to meet new clients in an effort to build my business into something greater. I wanted to truly thrive. I texted Danielle one last time after the seat belt sign was switched off upon arrival:

Thanks for an amazing time – I can't wait to see you back in Oz.

But the reality was that I didn't know if I would. As I watched the other passengers fussing about with their luggage, eager to stretch their legs, my heart felt like a table tennis ball that was being slammed back and forth in all directions. I just couldn't shake the feeling of loneliness – even after all that time in someone else's company. Was it an inherent flaw in me or was it the job? How on Earth could I still be depressed?

Coming back from Europe was like coming down after a binge. Life stayed exciting for a little while. I'll never forget walking the cobbled streets, drinking late-night cocktails in the cool bars and playing with gentle bondage exploration to the sway of the beautiful Tyrrhenian Sea. Back home, I mowed my ex's lawn, dealt with texts from people who had no intention of ever booking me and was generally just frustrated with everything. At least there was the vodka for when I truly felt alone. I figured that, if I was feeling the effects of an emotional come-down anyway, I might as well spend a couple of nights combatting jetlag with a few illicit substances in a valiant effort to get my sleep cycle back in sync with local time. When that didn't seem to work, I managed to try harder until I was a complete and utter mess and then I'd sleep for way too long. After a while, though, I finally headed back to the gym in an attempt to lose the weight that some of those European breakfast pastries had added to my belly, as well as to get my mind back in some sort of sexy state so I could forge on with work.

Did other people live like this? I thought about a parent/teacher interview at the school my son would be starting in a few weeks and I wondered how his teacher would judge me. Would she see straight through me? Would she see me as the loser I was? If I was going to champion sex work as a viable, meaningful and proud occupation, why did I taint it with the typical scenario of drug use and drunkenness? Could I be a male escort and not feel the need to dull my feelings on my days off? I wondered what was *really* wrong with me and whether sex work was helping or just making things worse.

Danielle was sending me texts telling me how much she missed me and I truthfully wrote back telling her I felt the same way. The bottom line, though, was that I didn't want to hurt her, as I knew I certainly wasn't ready to fall in love with anyone. I needed to love myself first.

And that was a lifelong struggle I wasn't sure I was ever going to achieve.

Chapter 41 –
More Issues with the Protocol

It'd been a couple of days since our last booking and the text messages between us included an attempt to make arrangements for me to collect some money I was owed. When the day came, however, she cancelled and said she was feeling sick – and because I was struggling to hide my irritation, I texted back.

Sorry, I'll just be off the phone for a bit. I'm a bit grumpy today.

Later that day, however, she texted again and told me we could meet at a local park near her place. I had my son with me, so after I was paid, we stayed in the park for a while before we all walked back to her door. Sam told me she was sorry she made me wait for my payment, that her ex-husband was making financial arrangements difficult and that she never meant to annoy me or let me down.

'You're not letting me down,' I told her. 'I know none of this is easy for you.'

She nodded but in a vague way. Her drifting had become more noticeable recently. I felt the bulge of the cash she'd handed me in my pocket and immediately felt awful that I had even gone there to take her money, not to mention being annoyed at the delay.

The nurturer inside me just wanted to help, but the survivor in me rationalised about how I would never have even met her if she hadn't wanted my professional services in the first place. It was an internal fight that continually made my gut lurch. That wasn't the way I imagined my life as a male escort would be. Real life, real emotions and real consequences were in the way, again – like they always seemed to be. I said goodbye with a hug and watched as she closed the door. As soon as I was alone with my son again, I looked at my beautiful little man, imagined the infinite possibilities of his young life and felt keenly aware that he soaked up every action and reaction I made. I immediately felt an overwhelming sense of responsibility. I hoisted him up on my shoulders and thought about rehab again.

The admissions nurse took a week too long to get back to me and in that time, I got cold feet. I couldn't do it. Not again. I reminded myself that daddy duty is my singular most important role and thought that *that* could be my motivation to quit. I could never, ever fuck that up. I knew I could be stronger than my addictions. I *had* to be stronger.

The following morning, Sam's friend called me. She was raising her voice to me again and asking me to explain why I took Sam out the day before without advising anyone.

'YOU KNOW ABOUT THE PROTOCOL!' she shouted. 'WHY DIDN'T FOLLOW IT?!'

When Sam suggested meeting me in the park that was just down the road from her house that day, I was too focused on the money I was owed to think about whether or not I needed to advise her carers she was stepping outside for ten minutes. Being out of her care loop was hard and because I only saw her intermittently, keeping up with how her illness was progressing was also becoming difficult to track.

She still lived alone, although I knew her carers visited her each day to help with her meals and chores, so I hadn't realised ten minutes in a nearby park would be such a problem – especially when I always escorted her back home and made sure she made it safely inside. I guess I just didn't think – and it was pretty stupid of me. Her friend was also concerned about something else Sam told her – in the company of her GP, as well – that I didn't use condoms when we had sex. I hadn't even had my first coffee of the day and this conversation just felt combative – I was beginning to feel bullied. And I don't react well to bullies.

'That's just bullshit,' I told her. 'I always use condoms, but the other day, it came off afterwards. I quickly put another one on as soon as it was needed.'

Why the fuck was I even telling her this? I felt like I was betraying Sam's dignity and it just felt wrong.

'Anyway,' I said, 'I don't want to go into the details of my private time with Sam but just know that I take my safety and health very seriously. It's everything in my job.'

There was silence at the other end of the line. It felt like she was judging me, but maybe she also realised this really was a huge invasion of not only Sam's privacy but also mine.

'Make sure it doesn't happen again,' she said.

She added 'please' after a pause, presumably to soften her tone, but the jolt of it had already stung.

I felt like the hired whore I was, and now I had someone insinuating that I was unprofessional and unclean. I ignored her last little dig, said, 'Okay, have a good one,' managed not to add 'bitch,' and hung up before she could respond.

Even in my world, it felt too early for vodka, so I gathered my stuff and headed to the gym. Sometimes, that helped as well.

Chapter 42 –
Trouble In Paradise

Things were feeling heavy and sometimes it felt like all I could think about was how Sam would be as she neared the end, as opposed to how she was right now. I didn't think of it as catastrophising though, as her demise was a forgone conclusion – the worst possible images I could imagine of her would definitely be realised and it would be up to me to decide when to bail out. It weighed me down, but not everything was all doom and gloom. At times, it felt like the gods smiled upon me and acknowledged the burden I sometimes carried by throwing me the odd bone here and there. About a week after my confrontation with Sam's friend, I received a message from one of my favourite Brisbane regulars. She said she had a work conference in Noosa and she was hoping I'd meet her up there for the last day of it. I was so excited – I could've practically sprinted up there!

I made the decision to fly instead and I arrived on the final Sunday morning of her conference. She finished her work duties around midday and from then on, it was all just sunbaking and sex. I'll never forget the image of my client as she was lying next to me face-down on a towel, with her golden skin slick with sweat and sunscreen and her bikini top undone across her back.

From my position on the deck chair, I drank in the view. It'd been a magnificent afternoon and I felt completely at peace.

We were the only ones by the pool and the only sounds I could hear were the swish of the afternoon breeze in the palm trees, and the call of small, colourful birds darting around the lawn. It was magical. At one point, as I hopped up to head to the bar, I noticed my phone ringing and saw that it was Sam. I was there for the beautiful woman beside me – and only her – and answering the phone to another client was most definitely a no-no. I quickly declined the call and put it on silent, but then it began vibrating. It was Sam again. I wondered if she'd made a mistake and didn't mean to call me, because she didn't leave a message or send a text, but when the phone rang a third time, I excused myself and told my client that I'd be back with some drinks in a few minutes.

I answered. 'Hey, Sam… what's up? Are you okay?'

She sounded annoyed – and a little bit scared.

'I've been buzzing and buzzing but you're not answering…'

I sat down on a stool near the bar and massaged my temples.

'You're at my door? At my place? Darling, I'm working in Queensland.'

I told her the truth of the situation – as I try to do whenever possible – and she told me she thought we had a date that evening.

'It's tomorrow, Sam. Today is Sunday. You're seeing me on Monday.'

There was silence for a good five seconds. She sounded really quiet. And embarrassed.

'Shit. I'm so sorry, Dan. I didn't mean to ruin your trip. I'll go now.'

I felt a bit bad for telling her that I was with another client but reassured her there'd been no harm done and I was just sorry that she got the days mixed up and made the effort to come to my place only to find me not there.

'But we're still on for tomorrow, aren't we?'

Her voice sounded even smaller when she replied. 'Sure. But now I have to get home.'

I visualised her standing in the entry foyer of my apartment building and I worried for a second. I told her to keep an eye on her phone and that I would call her an Uber, let the driver know that they would be picking her up and that I would screenshot the details to her. I could hear her relief.

'Thanks so much, Dan. I'm so sorry.'

Normally, if she came to my place for a booking, I'd drive her all the way home to make sure she made it back safely, so the thought of her waiting in the street and possibly getting into the wrong car made me anxious. I covered the phone for a second and ordered the drinks – two cosmos – and asked the waiter if he could bring them to us by the pool.

I quickly sorted out Sam's ride, sent her the screenshot and called her back to make sure she received it and knew which car to look out for.

'I'll text you in the morning to make sure we're all set for tomorrow night, okay?'

She still sounded really upset about it all. 'I'm so sorry. I feel like such a dick.'

I tried in vain to lighten the mood. 'Well, you'll have one tomorrow, darling!'

I'm not sure she got it, or more likely, she just didn't think it was funny. Which it wasn't. I stayed on the phone until she told me the car was approaching and I could hear the driver inviting her in. She thanked me again and said goodbye. I sent one last text asking her to let me know she'd arrived home safely, but she still sounded embarrassed when she replied.

I'm sorry I ruined your afternoon.

By the time I arrived back at the pool, our drinks had already been delivered. I said sorry to my client and told her the truth. I told her I had a client with early-onset Alzheimer's and she needed my help.

'Oh my God, was she okay?' she asked.

I reassured her that she was before we raised our glasses and celebrated the night ahead. Melbourne seemed so far away and I felt awful. I checked that my phone was still on silent, took another sip and walked to the edge of the pool before leaning over and diving in. The water was quite warm but it still felt refreshing, compared to the heat of my sun-soaked skin. We were having dinner soon, followed by a long night cuddling in bed together. The water had an energising effect and I rested my elbows on the edge of the pool to look at the gorgeous woman I was so lucky to be with, there in that tropical paradise. My concerns for Sam were already beginning to fade and I began to relax again. Every now and then, I had to pinch myself that the life I was living was real, but then just as quickly I would snap myself back into reality to prepare myself for another inevitable fall.

Chapter 43 – The Fellas

I'd lost track of how many texts I received from guys wondering if I provided services to men. My profile couldn't have made it more obvious that I only see women, but sometimes they weren't so keen to give up.

I'll pay double.

No, sorry, but thank you.

How about if we just watch porn and wank together?

No, sorry, but thank you.

My marketing pics worked well, and several fellas told me they loved the one with my bare chest showing from beneath my white shirt. I had to tell them I wouldn't change my mind, though – and that I really *was* straight – but that I was certainly flattered. And the truth is, I was. I wasn't interested in men and never have been, but what human doesn't like to feel appreciated by another?

Then there were the other calls involving guys who, apparently, wanted to watch me have sex with their girlfriends or wives in front of them as a cuckold sort of thing.

No. Sorry. One-on-one only.

Okay, so the truth is, I did feel a bit weird about the idea of some naked guy jerking off to the sight of me having sex with his wife, but I also didn't want to be in the middle of some relationship power-play where the reality of what went down would probably not match the client's expectations. My take on that was, if you had to add spark to your relationship by asking a second guy to do things to your partner that you couldn't do yourself, there could be a problem and my presence might make it worse. Instead of hiring me, I think those guys would be better off focusing on how they could do more to satisfy their partners – which meant talking to them more about their own bodies and properly listening to the ways they wanted to make love and be pleasured. I think a couple would be better off spending less on me and more on some fun sex toys or some new lingerie, or even some counselling to learn how best to reconnect with each other. I know of some wonderful people in the industry who help with things like that and couples counselling is something I'm interested in too. But then again – maybe I just have no idea how the whole group thing goes down, or the potential pleasure it brings them, because I've never done it. And nor will I. I have no interest in pleasuring men – even if they are a third party, and when I think about it, I want any partner I'm with to be focused only on me when we make love. But, I do acknowledge that, in this industry, that sounds pretty prudish and old-school.

I'd even gone so far as to meet up with couples to get a feel for them – just in case I thought I could pull it off – but it always made me feel anxious, so I said no. Personally, being in such close proximity to another naked man just hinders my libido, so I usually suggest they try other male escorts who specialise in couples and wish them a good time. I don't want to waste anyone's time or money, nor do I want to step on the toes of the other male escorts who genuinely enjoy providing those services – and a couple of them sound like they really get into it. Fortunately, the sex industry is an incredibly diverse and accommodating scene and, if you look hard enough, you will eventually find someone for everyone.

For conservative old Mitch, it's all about one-on-one attention and the reminder that we are all sexy in our own unique ways. I was glad my pics were working, though. When it comes to sex work advertising, photos are a powerful invitation and, as long as I kept myself looking good, I was hoping I'd be able to reap the rewards of this crazy career for a few more years to come. In the meantime, I hoped that revising my online profile by more clearly outlining my specific conditions would make it clear that I was there for women and women only, and for the people who kept trying to tempt me to the other side – that was still cool. I wouldn't change my mind but I wouldn't feel offended, either. Being seen as attractive in someone else's eyes was never a negative thing to me. And sometimes, it was an ego boost I needed to get through a rough day.

Chapter 44 —
Caravans, Cricket and Coming

My older woman was getting older. As we all were, of course.

She was passing through Adelaide before heading back to Perth and she wondered if we could make plans to meet up. I figured that she must've seen my post on Instagram, promoting the tour that I'd planned while the borders were still open. She gave me the address of a holiday park, of all places, and although the venue choice would be a first for me, I must admit that I wasn't in any hurry to experience it. But it wasn't me paying for the accommodation, so I agreed and put the details for an overnight booking in my calendar.

It'd been a while, so we chatted about the pandemic (as usual) before the topic switched to what she wanted me to do to her body the following week. I improvised and added my own suggestions, telling her that I couldn't wait to feel her lips on mine. I wondered if she believed me because I wasn't sure I believed myself.

I can get in the mood with almost any client when I close my eyes and focus on touch, so the barrier I was starting to feel between myself and this particular client was beginning to worry me. Had I lost my professional edge? I was proud of my ability to get genuinely immersed in every sexual moment I was a part of. It was a skill I'd honed and it helped my performance, which then helped the quality of my testimonials and my marketability. Also, it helped my sanity. If I couldn't pretend that I was enjoying it, I wondered how long I could do it without driving myself crazy. But every time I was with her, I'd been noticing a growing discomfort inside me like I was stepping over a societal line that was unacceptable and frowned upon.

Was I a freak? Or did it make me just seem like a mercenary hooker, who would do anything for a buck? I decided to stop thinking about it. I had a week to psych myself up for that booking and I was sure the fragility of my current mood had more to do with my usual over-indulgences and lack of sleep than it did with any actual reticence. I had to remember that she was an intelligent woman, who adored what I did with her, and I needed to go out of my way to adore her right back. Like a professional.

Age is meaningless, in the broader scheme of things. And she had been young once. I repeated the thought in my head – like a mantra – until I was practically convinced.

Age is meaningless. She was young once.

Age is meaningless. She was young once.

Time, however, kept ticking, and when the time arrived and I'd navigated my way through the airport arrival lounge and collected my hire car, I entered the address my client gave me into my phone. I'd made her my first booking and I'd sourced my own accommodation for the rest of my tour and chosen an expensive hotel in the CBD. At that point, though, my shiny little hatchback was heading towards the beachside caravan park she'd given me the address of and I called her quickly to let her know that I wasn't too far away.

There's nothing sexy about caravan parks – not when you're in your forties, your date is in her early seventies and you're in a cabin only metres away from where a family is arguing over the rules of Uno. Some kind of small dog was yapping into the night and, a few doors away, the drone of a cricket commentator on an old-school radio drifted through the air with the smell of sausages, greasy chops and onions sizzling on a barbecue somewhere. A little boy yelled at a little girl and the little girl yelled back. Some older kids passed by on bicycles, attempted some wheelies and pulled off some sweet skids. Meanwhile, my client was now sitting at the table under the fluorescent light, reaching one hand down to pull down the zip of my shorts.

'I want to feel you, Dan,' she whispered. 'Are you hard?'

I wasn't, actually, so I playfully wiggled my hips away from her as I tried my best to visualise some scenario that would help me get in the mood – anything that didn't have a barking dog, a bicycle bell, feuding siblings and an increasingly noisy card game in it.

I excused myself to go to the tiny bathroom to regroup. Once there, I looked at myself in the mirror and smiled. It calmed me down. I closed my eyes and reached into my shorts, grabbed myself and squeezed. It worked, slightly. So as not to arouse suspicion, I flushed the toilet and returned to the front area of the cabin. The 'living room', I suppose. I took a sip of cider, smiled and closed my eyes again before tracing my hand across her chest under her blouse. I could feel her nipple stiffen underneath my touch. My cock twitched again slightly.

'Shall we?' she suggested.

Her invitation came with a wave of her hand towards the rear of the cabin. In that setting, it required taking about eight big steps. I took her hand. The mattress felt terribly firm as I laid her down gently and unbuttoned the dress that had flattened itself against her skin.

'Would you like me to turn off the light again?'

She nodded, so I flicked the switch in the living room to see her silhouetted against the quilt cover as the evening light streamed in through one of the windows. We'd been together a few times, now. I knew her body and what made her quietly arch and groan and, although I was there for the whole night, I was conscious not to move too quickly – and she didn't complain. I closed my eyes again to focus on those senses, but the smell of onion and sausages was overpowering and I was struggling.

Meanwhile, at the cricket, someone was pretty convinced someone else was out – LB, by the sounds of it. I had to focus so I ran my tongue up the inside her leg and buried my face between her legs, hoping her moans would muffle the outside sounds, if only for a while. Within a few minutes, she was wriggling against my tongue and I moved it round and round until I guessed she was done. She was very quiet when she came, but I'd come to learn the signs. Muscles tensing then relaxing, breath rate increasing, then slowing. It was such a relief. She smiled at me and stroked my forehead and face.

'Your turn, my beautiful boy.'

She said it in such a beautiful, caring way that my hardness stunned me for a second. I kept my eyes closed while her mouth slid over me. I could still smell those sausages but as my pulse quickened and her face bobbed up and down against me, I realised that I was still well and truly in touch with my talent, to lose myself in the person I was with by turning a blind eye to the details. It's what kept me going – not just that day in the caravan park, but every other day I was with clients who didn't immediately make my heart race. But there were so many that did and at that moment, I thought of one in particular – Anna – until I saw her face and felt her mouth wrapped around me. I shuddered and pulled my client closer as I came. It was a beautiful experience ending with us stroking each other back to Earth, while our breathing slowed. Past experience with this client had taught me about her libido and I knew that was probably it for the night. I pictured myself trying to sleep next to her with the buzzing of the mosquito zapper outside and the sound of people shuffling to the communal toilet block in the dark, and knew it would going to be a long night and I needed sleep for my other clients. I didn't want to be there but that is exactly where I was, so once again, I focused on the moment to relax myself – that strange moment in that Big 4 Caravan Park – and I smiled.

I rolled towards her and looked her in the eye as I stroked her hair.

'That was fantastic.' She giggled.

I gave her my best attempt at a sexy smile and kissed her cheek.

'*You're* fantastic,' I whispered.

She leaned into me and touched my chest before her fingers made their way further down between my legs. My cock jumped beneath her fingers.

She smiled. 'So are you.'

Chapter 45 – The Convert

Organising a tour to another city was usually about picking up as many quality bookings as I could physically manage, in the shortest possible amount of time. I always prioritised my beloved regular clients but I also looked forward to meeting new ones. Many of them admitted to following me on social media for many months before finally taking the plunge and contacting me after seeing that I was heading their way. It was a hell of a privilege to be able to pick and choose which city I visited, and I often pinched myself – wondering who this bloke was that these beautiful women were interested in meeting, and finding it hard to believe it was little old me. To say I sometimes tended to suffer from a bit of imposter syndrome here and there would be a huge understatement.

My 'mature' client was a regular, but the woman who responded to my Instagram post announcing my trip to Adelaide told me that she was a first-timer. In more ways than one. She said that she was in a same-sex marriage and had been for nine years. Just recently though, she explained, she'd had an overwhelming feeling that tingled inside her in a way that was impossible to ignore any longer. She wanted to try being with a man again. She had only ever been with one when she was quite young and felt comfortable taking the leap with me after reading the testimonials my other amazing clients had left for me. We flirted on the phone for a few days before meeting and she offered to send me a photo, which is something I always appreciated. She was a beautiful full-figured blonde with slightly Polynesian features and after seeing her picture, I started to get quite excited. I checked my calendar and asked her if the following Sunday would suit her. I planned to see her the day after my overnighter in the caravan park. She told me that she'd arrange a hotel room for us and would let me know where to meet her.

There were a lot of thoughts racing through my head after that. Most of them were those pesky new client nerves, which seemed to start as soon as a booking was made, but I was also curious about her situation. I wondered if her partner even knew of her secret desire or if their own version of setting boundaries around this fantasy was to make this happen under someone else's roof – in a similar way as the heterosexual couples I'd met. Thinking of your partner being with somebody else can mean different things to different people, but I imagine that when you're queer and your long-term partner suddenly talks about wanting to be with someone of the opposite sex, a sense of concern and an inability to compete might cause potential issues. Nevertheless, in the days before our booking, I texted her again – partly to see if she was still committed, and partly to start the slow tease that I hoped would bring both of us to the booking with confidence.

It was one of those inner-city 'arty' hotels – nothing too over-the-top but clean, slick and contemporary. She'd already told me about the bar just two doors away and we agreed to meet there for a few cocktails to kick the evening off. I was already there when she arrived and she approached me at the bar with a very sexy and disarming giggle. She had a retro style about her, with a couple of tattoos, several earrings in each ear and the ubiquitous black clothes that gave her an air of graphic designer cool. Two drinks later, she suggested we go up to the room. I felt a sense of relief that seeing me in the flesh hadn't made her change her mind. She'd already checked in, so when we walked into the suite, I noticed that the lights were already dimmed and the champagne bucket on the coffee table had two flutes next to it, ready to help us continue the party mood. It was good champagne, too, and after a glass each, the flirting was reaching fever pitch. I leaned in towards her as she rested against the arm of the couch.

'I'm dying to kiss you. Can I?'

She nodded and leant into me.

Her lips were full and soft, and her tongue began probing – a little more than I'd have liked, but still manageable. She never told me what her experience was like with that man (boy, really) all those years ago, but the way her hand found my crotch, I sensed a certain familiarity. Her grip was firm as she cupped my balls and her thumb circled me through my pants as her other hand reached up to stroke my chest. I asked her if she enjoyed oral sex. She laughed.

'What do you think?'

Feeling a bit stupid, I knelt down in front of the couch and pushed her skirt up over her hips. I took off her lacy, black underwear and started kissing and nibbling her inner thigh. She giggled in a very adorable way. I then flicked my tongue against her slowly, teasing her. Her hands reached behind my head and pulled me in harder. I could already taste her and knew that there was no need for me to reach for the lube. I looked up at her as I gently slipped my finger inside her. Her head was tilted back while she unzipped her dress from behind to give her large breasts more room. It took a few more minutes before I felt her reach the edge of her orgasm; she pushed my face harder between her legs as she trembled and moaned.

'Oh my God,' she panted. 'You're fucking *good*.'

Because I didn't know exactly how far she wanted to go, I decided to let her lead the way and as I stood up again and sat back on the couch, her hand reached for me. I then lifted my hips, helped her pull down my pants and held my cock in anticipation.

'Would you mind?' I asked.

I was looking forward to her answer; the idea of a woman who normally chooses women being so keen to explore my body was turning me on in a way I wasn't expecting. She knelt down and took me in her hands, then her mouth and when she looked up at me to ask how she was doing, I just stroked her hair, smiled and groaned with genuine pleasure. She was doing just fine. After a while, I sensed that she wanted to feel me inside her and I was very happy to oblige – taking it slowly at first, then harder as she pushed against me.

'This is so bloody good...' She said it almost as a scream and it was all I needed to hear to make me explode. It was sooner than usual for me but the timing felt natural so I just allowed myself to let go.

'Oh my God,' she said afterwards. 'That was incredible.'

I was loving the compliments and I thanked her.

I needed a bit of a break to recharge but we were both definitely up for more, so we had a shower and a few more drinks before continuing. When our three-hour session was officially up and I said goodbye, she promised that she would be in touch again and asked me when I was planning my next trip. I told her that she would be the first to know. We kissed at the door one last time and once again I found myself walking down another hotel hallway, with another envelope of cash in my little bag and a happy client soon to become a lovely memory. It's moments like that when I felt strangely connected to other sex workers worldwide, actually. How many of us went through a similar routine that night? How many of us felt the same nerves beforehand and the same feelings of relief and satisfaction afterwards?

Not all bookings are like that, though, and I knew it was only a matter of time before another stressful one came along to keep my confidence and ego in check. But at that time, I felt wonderful, and I wanted to kick on. As I was quite familiar with Adelaide, I knew of a fun pub I could go to in Hindley Street, just near my hotel, where I could have a few more drinks and blow some cash to celebrate what had been a very interesting and very successful tour.

Chapter 46 – On Retainer

Discussing how often Sam needed to have sex was a weird conversation to have with her sister, who I'd never actually met. It wasn't the first time she and I had chatted but as Sam's condition worsened, and the financial issues between her and her ex-husband became more apparent, her sister stepped up into her role as power of attorney to help Sam manage her final years with some dignity and happiness – and that included negotiating rates and regularity with the male escort she wanted to see.

I loved that her sister cared so much that she included me on her list of important things needed to help Sam find some happiness. I was sure it made her more awkward than it made me. I mentioned the issue that had been bugging me at times – of how Sam's forgetfulness sometimes meant that I didn't get paid – so we came up with a less stressful arrangement for everyone. A monthly amount that was paid, like clockwork – and she assured me she would manage it, so there wouldn't be any more errors. Then, without all the precise details, we talked about what I would be delivering in return – a combination of social dates, as well as longer bookings to allow me to fulfil Sam's sexual needs. I felt good. The feeling that I was making a positive difference to someone's life was something I needed that morning, especially after the previous night's bloody awful booking with some random who'd met me at her door with a greasy ponytail, tracksuit pants and a slice of pizza before demanding I come upstairs to 'get started'.

Being an escort was nothing that I thought it would be like. For a few weeks, work might've been absolute heaven and I could do no wrong. At times like that, I felt I was destined to please and could do it forever. Then, in the blink of an eye, in the following week, it could be degrading and gross and I would become incredibly anxious about what my future might look like if I quit. Back then, when I thought about how Sam's sister acknowledged my skills and my ability to help her, it felt special in a way that made my heart swell. I felt like a true caregiver; a man with a higher purpose who used his mind and body to make someone else's life a little bit more manageable. It was a great feeling, so I put the dates Sam's sister and I discussed in my calendar to help map out the months ahead.

Finally, I felt like a real professional who was doing something to be proud of. I poured myself a vodka and tonic, raised my glass to nobody and felt that wonderful cold spirit wash across my tongue. It felt so nice to be needed – and even better to be respected.

Chapter 47 –
The Reveal – Second Attempt

There was no easy way I could tell my parents that I was a sex worker.

In the end, I approached it head-on. They were confused about my recent trip overseas and doubted I was making enough as a photographer to survive, so I thought it best to come clean. In the build-up, I could tell that Dad had already raced to the conclusion that I was 'coming out' in a different sense but I explained that no, that wasn't the case.

In the fantasy version of me telling them about my job, I imagined Dad and I bonding and laughing, with him joking about how much sex I was getting and how he thought I was one of the luckiest guys he knew. But that's not what happened. Acknowledgement is one step but acceptance is something that's much, much bigger and, really, I wasn't sure if Mum and Dad would ever go that far. I knew they wanted 'more' for me, but what they needed to understand was that this is what I wanted for myself. I thought they probably saw it as some frivolous, dirty attempt of mine to get as much sex from as many different people as possible and it made me sad to think of them wondering where they went wrong. Nothing went wrong, Mum – and even if it did, and I am somehow broken inside, none of it is your fault. But I do genuinely feel happier than I have in a very long time.

I told them as many details as I thought they could process, over a cup of tea, in an attempt to normalise the confession that they'd been confronted with. I willed them to ask me for details so I could have the opportunity to tell them what my life was really like. I needed them to understand that the images of late-night hook-ups in seedy hotel rooms with hats and dark sunglasses were not realistic and I made it clear to them that I only saw my clients one-on-one, in romantic, loving environments and that above all, I was safe. I wanted to tell them about the women who valued me – that some women chose me to help them heal emotional injuries from their past and that some women told me that I helped their spirits soar, even if it was just for a short amount of time. I wanted to tell them about the women who had been hurt, who found it hard to trust, and about the women who found it hard to love themselves. Above all, I wanted to assure them that I was still a good son and a good dad, even if the truth was that, maybe, I was never much good at being a husband.

I told them my ex wife knew, and the surprise that registered on my mother's face was obvious but she didn't press me for more details. That overseas trip I went on? That was a booking – someone flew me there to travel with them to be their date at a business conference. Mum just nodded quietly while Dad just fiddled with his cup – probably worrying about Mum. In the end, I pleaded with them to at least read a few of my testimonials so they could truly understand what I did – from the horse's mouth.

After a while, I just stopped talking. I could tell they didn't want to hear any more and I knew I needed to give them space to process just how little they knew about their son. I longed for the day they might have felt comfortable enough to ask me about specific bookings or about my clients or about how I ran my business, but I knew that would be a long time coming – if ever.

I couldn't push them anymore. At the time, I was convinced that I didn't care who knew what I was doing and that I was proud of it, but at that moment, and to an extent, ever since, all I felt was an overwhelming feeling of shame. Their son, a former lawyer and happily married man, had officially reached rock bottom and was selling his body to survive. Mum especially looked really uncomfortable. I imagined us all at Christmas, with the extended family present, everyone tiptoeing around the elephant in the room and I understood her fears. That stigma and lack of understanding about sex work wasn't going anywhere. I sighed and told her that ultimately, I was happy and safe. I hoped that was what she needed to hear but all she did was nod at me, then excuse herself to leave the room. Dad sat there for a moment but didn't say anything. Which was unusual for him.

'Do you want a hand mowing the lawn?'

He nodded and gave me a grateful smile. 'Sure, Daniel. That'd be great.'

I followed him through the house to the backyard and got the mower out. As I paced up and down across the lawn, cutting stripes into the long, soft grass, I was grateful for their love and support, even if it wasn't shown in ways that were as obvious as I'd have liked. I didn't know how I expected them to react, but I was very, very relieved that my secret was out. I thought that all I could realistically do was just continue being their son, and maybe chat to them more often. I was glad they didn't seem devastated by the news, but I also wished they would say what they really thought so we could properly clear the air. Small steps, though. That was one huge confession made.

The next one I was still thinking about tackling was how to tell them that I might have an addiction issue that needed dealing with. I decided I'd give myself a little longer to sort that one out myself, though.

Chapter 48 – Sally

Why would a smart, professional and utterly gorgeous woman need to hire an escort to have her sexual needs met?

Like I've said, many things in this industry remain a mystery to me but in the meantime, I was ecstatic that Sally chose me and became one of my biggest and most pleasurable reasons to stay in the game.

She was simply wonderful. She was approaching fifty but had the body of a very fit thirty-year-old. She loved the same dance music as I did and in terms of physical attraction, I thought her long, thick blonde hair was gorgeous. She usually dressed down in a bohemian sort of way, and it suited her perfectly. I was particularly fond of the flimsy summer dresses she used to wear as it allowed me to immediately feel her sublime physique the minute we saw each other to kiss and embrace. Sally also had an adorably childish and cheeky attitude to almost everything life threw at her – made even more attractive by her cute little button nose and wonderful laugh. If I sound like I was a fan, it's because I was. We'd somehow managed to create an ideal bubble of a relationship that set it apart from any other interaction I'd had. It wasn't a traditionally romantic relationship because, at the start of each 'date', she handed me an envelope containing cash with a lovely card and paid me for my time. It wasn't a traditional provider/client relationship, either. Both of us blurred the boundaries very early on, and it became so different, and so special, that we didn't even know what we were meant to call it. But here's a word, for starters: *fun*. I had so much fun with Sally. We sometimes started each booking with a few lines of coke, or maybe some MDMA, after which we would drink and talk incessantly about our lives. We danced, we made love, we laughed and then we'd do it all over again – and usually for at least five hours or more. She'd truly come to feel like one of my best friends.

The next word I think of when I picture Sally? *Insatiable*.

Make that *exhaustingly* insatiable.

If anyone decided to produce an adult version of an illustrated dictionary and they were looking for the ideal image to describe 'insatiable', there would need to be a picture of her, lying naked on the bed of her inner-city apartment, positively writhing, with her beautiful butt pointing up in the air, begging to be taken. Sally loved sex and – lucky me – she especially loved Mitch. Actually, she loved Dan, and she came to know me very well.

Our first booking was incredible. I put it down to the fact that it came off the back of weeks of flirty phone conversations, where I was able to glean a thorough understanding of what turned her on and how I could satisfy her beyond anything she'd ever felt before. If practice really did make perfect, I was well past racking up the necessary hours that made me a bonafide expert and Sally was a willing recipient of my knowledge. For Sally, it was all about touch and stimulation – constant and consistent. I'd learned my lesson from being with her in person several times, that preparation for one of her bookings required the kind of training an athlete would do before a big game.

Sexually, she was hard work. There were no shortcuts. I always left there feeling completely spent both physically and emotionally and, because our meetings also usually involved a couple of sneaky lines washed down with homemade cocktails just to add to the debauchery, I always caught Ubers home. Those rides flew by, too. I clearly remember how every muscle in my body seemed to tingle with a special kind of warmth after seeing her and I would just float along in timeless bliss before arriving back at my apartment in what seemed like no time at all.

After a while, it even got to the stage where I needed to block out the days on either side of our booking to rest. I was a fit and reasonably healthy guy, but I sometimes found that I struggled to keep up. If I'd had a big one the night before, there was no way I could keep pace with her and I'd even stopped doing my afternoon workout if I was seeing her that night. I knew I needed to save my strength. It wasn't just the sex that made my muscles ache, either. Sally was one of the smartest, funniest people I'd met and I'd often laugh so much, my stomach ached too.

After a while, and in between our fortnightly bookings, the frequency of our phone calls began to increase. Because she was always keen to do the right thing by me, she often paid me for video calls, in between all those other hot texts we exchanged for free. At one stage, however, I remember her asking me questions about my other clients and although I tried to play it down, I sensed that she was becoming increasingly uncomfortable about my feelings for my other regular clients. To me, her jealousy was flattering, but there was always a part of me which felt guilty, too. I care for all my clients and I'm protective of them – as well as being respectful of my feelings for them. But what was I starting to feel for Sally? And what was she already feeling for me? It's one of the dangers of regular sex work, whether you're male or female. Humans who get familiar with each other start to care more. And just how deep that care can go is something that sometimes needs to be carefully monitored.

Sally came with her own boundary which, I feel, managed to keep things light and manageable though – she was in a long-term, open relationship. Her partner sounded like a really kind and loving man too. Not only because he was someone she adored, but also because he was aware of the situation between us. Out of respect for each other, they didn't discuss any details of the flings they had, which was beneficial given how often she booked me, but sometimes, when Sally was particularly self-conscious or vulnerable, I secretly wondered how hard it would be when the time came that we were forced to say goodbye. Whenever those feelings of doubt and concern crept in though, I'd consciously snap myself out of it, remember how amazing my life was and focus more on how incredibly lucky I was to have been chosen by her.

Chapter 49 – Yee Har!

Around the time I first met Sally, I connected with another new client. She seemed nice enough – a bit geeky looking, but in a very sexy way, giving off an almost standoffish, corporate vibe, complete with heavy-framed dark glasses, a knee-length skirt and a cardigan she pulled over a nice body-hugging, floral blouse. And not unlike Sally, she said that she loved being on top. I had a feeling that beneath that quiet-looking exterior, there was a confident, sexual woman who knew what she liked and knew how to make herself happy, and she was going to give me one hell of a run for my (or should I say her) money. I was quite happy to oblige, though. In fact, I probably would have been quite happy to oblige for free, for that matter.

She intrigued me mentally as well as physically and I was already feeling my suit pants bulge. Her dark, meticuously straightened hair fell just below her shoulders and the way in which she suductively swept her long fringe away from her glasses during our initial conversation appeared deliberately flirtatious and very effective. I'd chosen a semi-formal look that night. From the conversations we had, and the pic she sent of herself inside her townhouse, I had her pegged as a woman of style who would appreciate a well-dressed man. The combination of my light grey suit combined with a simple white shirt with no tie, and a touch of fake tan, made my skin look healthy and slightly sun-kissed. She had a great taste in music and it didn't take long for the mood to shift and the air to feel somehow warmer. I'd been stroking her hair as I sat across from her on the couch and I asked if it was okay to kiss her. I answered her nod by leaning towards her and feeling my lips brush against hers.

She was quite petite and all the right curves were tight against the material of her blouse in a most magnificent way. I ran my hand gently along across her neck and started to undo her top button as we kissed. Then button number two. And three. After I removed her cardigan and as her blouse slipped up over her head, her gorgeous chest was revealed. I ran my tongue between her breasts as I traced around her lacy white bra cup. I reached behind her to remove her bra and caught one breast on my mouth as it tumbled free – which she loved. She pulled me back towards the couch and lay down, inviting me to lay on top of her. I was as hard as a rock by then, which I'm sure she could feel through my pants.

'Let's get rid of these, shall we?' I suggested.

She tugged at my zip and I helped her pull them down. I rolled over, grabbed a condom and slid it on in record time. She motioned for me to lay down on the couch and positioned herself above me, with one hand reaching between her legs to pull her underwear aside as she slid down over me. She groaned. As did I. That first contact was the best feeling ever.

'I told you I like being on top.'

She was nibbling my ear as she whispered it and it sounded incredibly hot. I kissed her neck when she leaned into me as I felt the warmth of being inside her. Irritatingly, the couch wasn't comfortable at all, and her enthusiasm was pounding me harder and harder against the barely padded timber arm until my back felt tenderised and possibly bruised from all the pressure. I had to call a time out.

'Hey, can we move to the bed?'

She nodded and got up from the couch, so I followed her. I sat her down on the edge of the bed and started doing what I always love – oral.

'Can I sit on your face?'

Okay, so she likes being on top for that as well, I thought. *Fine by me.*

I shimmied my body back across the mattress and she slid her thighs around my head and lowered herself over my waiting mouth. My moan was muffled, but hers was getting louder and as she got more and more into it; her rhythm became a heavy, steady grind, back and forth as my head pushed hard against the mattress. I was seriously struggling to breathe, however, and was getting flashbacks from the psycho who almost suffocated me, but managed to time it so I could take deep breaths every few seconds – like I was swimming. Finally, and when I could speak, I asked her if we could change positions.

'But I'm so close! Please don't stop.'

The customer is always right, I thought, so I lay on the bed again as she resumed her grinding. When she eventually came, her thighs squeezed tight around my head and I was trapped temporarily until I felt the last tremble of her body. I was gasping for air, but super chuffed with myself at the same time. Being suffocated was much better this time around. I gently extracted myself from between her legs – keen to rehydrate. But she was already wanting more.

'Let's finish what we started on the couch.'

So, I ended up on my back again, with her hips grinding down against me, and I had to put my hands on her hips to slow her down so I didn't come, or break my back – or both. She moved into a wide rotation and I felt like I was going to snap inside her. I pulled her back into line again and tried to keep her steadier, as well as trying to keep me inside her. There's nothing worse than slipping completely out, then having the full weight of a client's body crunch down on your hard penis. It'd happened before and it cost me a future booking.

Up and down. Up and down. I had my eyes closed and face buried in her neck in an attempt to put my mind elsewhere so as not to come and after a while, she finally climaxed again as my fingers tightly gripped her arse cheeks.

I was exhausted and absolutely drenched in sweat. It wasn't because of her weight at all – it was due to the rapid pace and her technique, and as a woman who clearly knew what position pleased her, she'd obviously spent a lot of time working on both. It was almost too much for me. Or maybe it was just the combination of that afternoon's workout, that terribly uncomfortable couch and seeing Sally earlier that week.

The booking wasn't over yet, though, and after getting us both a drink, she was back – and she wanted to be on top again. Thank God I'd held off coming. I obliged again, but tried to hold on to her hips a little more firmly this time, controlling her speed and her force so I didn't feel as though I was a piece of schnitzel being tenderised. She seemed to be super happy and so was I. After some more light oral and some more traditional sex, I rolled off her and pulled the quilt up over her sweaty body.

'Oh my God.' She gasped. 'That was the best.'

And I agreed.

She leaned over to kiss my cheek. I was glowing with pride. But now there was a new problem and I was worried that I couldn't get up without looking like a decrepit old man. A muscle in my lower back felt tight and pinched, and even rolling to one side made me wince in agony. I couldn't even cough without feeling searing pain shoot across my hips. I didn't want her to see me like that and I felt embarrassed about the damage her favourite position has caused my battered body. I asked her if she'd mind grabbing me a drink before I left and she leapt out of bed, happy to oblige.

'I'll just get dressed and meet you in the kitchen.'

As I said it, I was worried that my voice was somehow straining and I waited for her to grab the robe she had hanging on the end of her bed and leave, before I rolled myself off the bed and thudded to the floor.

'Ugh!' I winced. God, it really hurt.

I coughed to try and cover it up – but that just caused more pain. Hunched over in pain and still naked on the floor, I managed to bundle up my clothes, held onto the bed and painfully stood. After trying in vain to stretch out the injury, I hobbled to the bathroom and used the toilet seat as a stool to rest each leg on as I pulled my pants on and then buttoned up my shirt. I could barely lift my legs; my back felt as though it was on fire. I tried not to limp as I made my way to the kitchen to find her there, with a huge smile, holding out a glass of icy water. I thanked her and drank it while she was in the bathroom and then we said our goodbyes.

After gingerly lowering my battered body into my car, I managed to make it home. Once there, I sent her the usual follow up text and she messaged back saying she would love to see me again in exactly two weeks. I told her I'd check my calendar and let her know early the next morning. First things first, though – I needed to run a hot bath, take some ibuprofen and collapse into bed. *And next time,* I thought, *I'll insist we mix it up a bit, so I don't end up in a fucking wheelchair.*

Chapter 50 – My Favourite Thing

I never thought that being a male escort would be a potentially dangerous occupation, but having highly active sex – sometimes several times a week – came with its own unique type of wear and tear that affected both your body and your mind.

I'd been scratched, cut, bitten, squashed, squeezed, and one night, I even watched bright red blood drip into the shower cubicle after that night's client had cut my anus with one of her fingernails during a particularly exploratory lovemaking session. I didn't invite just anyone to get that involved, of course, but when I was having sex with some of my regular clients, the need to ramp things up would often lead to a bit of experimentation and boundary-pushing.

I've allowed myself to be 'pegged' by a friend and I've shoved butt plugs up myself – in order to have the confidence to do the same thing to any given client who requested it. Knife, needle or even rope play isn't my cup of tea because to me, even before I became Mitch, there was so much excitement in 'regular' sex that I never found the need to partake in anything too extreme. I liked to think that my skill was in working with the very basics and then raising the bar to higher levels of pleasure using emotions and body language. I liked to start with the simple things, such as eye contact and smiling, followed by verbal flirting, then eventually kissing, teasing and gentle stroking. Penetrative sex is amazing, of course, but it doesn't have to be the pinnacle, and when you start to truly lose yourself in each other's bodies, the sex gets better and better every single time, in many different ways.

Familiarity can sometimes lead to boredom, of course, but it can also allow you to start at a point that would otherwise take a long time to reach. And where you go from there is only limited by your imagination and patience. I believe that the best possible sex takes place when lovers are so attuned to each other's emotions that they can virtually play each other like instruments. Oral sex plays a huge role in that and (surprise, surprise) is one of my favourite things to do in bed. To me, everything about it is a turn-on. It's the most personal, private space for a woman and if you're invited to go there, it feels like you've been given the keys to a wonderful kingdom. For me, the simple act of kissing is a similar privilege, but having the permission to kiss a woman between her legs and being allowed to have your face pressed close against her is the best feeling of all. Fingers can do amazing things, too, and if you combine them with just the right amount of pressure in the right areas, the combination of tongue, lips and fingers is a perfect match. To me, the act of oral is the ultimate way to give pleasure and, provided your partner feels completely uninhibited and safe, is the easiest way to bring a woman to orgasm. I find the whole learning process a huge turn-on, too. I love trying different pressures, movements and speeds to see what works for each particular client. It's incredibly enjoyable and always a lot of fun.

Another thing I've heard from my clients is that a lot of men they encounter don't seem to enjoy pleasing their partners that way, or possibly, they aren't inclined to learn. As a consequence, many of the women I've spoken to feel embarrassed to ask for it as much as they'd like to. A further issue can arise when they do find a partner happy to please them, they may be hesitant to clearly direct them to their special spots – so they either fake pleasure for their partner's sake or they abandon the whole exercise altogether.

I can relate to this. As strange as this sounds coming from a man, I don't usually like receiving oral sex myself. Especially from a new client. It's a bit of an issue for me too, as women are generally very eager to please me in return for my efforts and can be quite offended if I gently guide them away. In my screwed up, escorting mind, I feel pressured to remain hard during oral sex and if I find myself going soft, I feel I'm letting my lover down. Strange, isn't it? There are lots of sexual mysteries that don't make a whole lot of sense to me, but I love figuring them out along the way with clients I can trust and who trust me. Ultimately, if I can help someone else feel proud of their body, or if I can help them feel more empowered and comfortable with asking for exactly what they want and how they want it, I'll be a happy man.

Well, happier, at least.

Chapter 51 –
More Confusion. More Questions.

Although Sam and I hadn't seen each other for weeks, her text messages suddenly started arriving in my inbox with greater frequency. When I read them, I felt a rising knot in the pit of my stomach. She sounded different. Confused. One day, she texted to book a coffee date with me and the next day, she texted again with the same request – repeated – and seemed short with me when I wrote back to tell her we'd already set the date. I immediately felt guilty about both pointing out her error and then feeling annoyed at the way she responded. I read somewhere that when someone is suffering from Alzheimer's, it's always best to just play along and pretend that topics had not already been discussed. It was the polite way of going about things and it made life much more tolerable for the person suffering from the disease. Communication by text has a way of making a polite correction sound like frustration, so I chided myself for not being more patient with Sam and her failing memory. I recall that I was in a supermarket queue at the time and I chose to respond to her immediately instead of taking the time to think for a while before choosing my words more carefully. I vowed to hold off and respond with no distractions next time.

I'm sorry, darling, I texted. *I shouldn't have mentioned it. I can't wait to see you on Thursday.*

But on Thursday morning, another text from Sam arrived to tell me about a family friend who was coming to stay with her and how it just wasn't going to work out that day.

A week later, on a Friday morning, I received another text asking if I could meet her for coffee later that afternoon. She had forgotten that her ex was taking the kids away for the weekend with his girlfriend. She said she was at a loose end and was trying to distract herself from the sadness of being alone the whole time – and I could certainly relate. I already had a booking unfortunately, but because I didn't want to talk about other clients, I told her that my son had an event at school that I needed to go to. But then I kicked myself again. In my rush to give her an excuse of why I couldn't see her, I ended up talking about my own access to my child when what was upsetting her was her lack of access to her own. I felt like I was tiptoeing blindfolded through a minefield. I told her that I was sorry and asked if there was another day we could be together.

How about Sunday?

She didn't reply.

I waited a couple of hours and sent the message again, with an extra note asking if she'd got my message the first time. And then she called me.

'Hi there, lovely!' I answered. 'How are you?'

Her response sounded quiet, slow and maybe a bit irritated. 'Did we have a booking on Sunday?'

Her obvious confusion caught me by surprise and my emotions quickly shifted gears to hide my worry for her, whilst also hiding the burning annoyance that I felt about yet another booking mix-up. Patience is a virtue I've always found challenging to practice. In this case, I was torn between running my business as Mitch and the empathetic part of Dan, who saw this woman as someone who was facing an unimaginable void. I was starting to seriously doubt whether I could help her through it or even if I was the right person to be involved at this late stage of her once-vibrant life. I closed off the conversation by telling her that I would be more than happy to see her on Sunday, if that suited her.

'I'd really love to see you, Sam. I've missed you.' And I meant it.

On my days off, it was either Sam or my little family that I thought of. Since outing myself to my parents, I'd instinctively ostracised myself and saw them rarely. I kidded myself by pretending it was because I was too busy but deep down, I knew it was the shame. I was glad my ex didn't have to keep quiet any longer, though, and could now lean on my parents for more support with my boy while I travelled for work.

There were no silver linings with Sam, though. The day would come – and sooner rather than later – when she wouldn't be able to recognise her kids. I imagined, long before that, I'd also become one of the fuzzy memories that would no longer hold meaning in her life. She wasn't there yet, but I knew it was coming. Now that we'd finally settled on the Sunday for our next meeting, I imagined her reaching for the red biro that sat on her special 'memory' bench in the kitchen, which she would use to record everything in the oversized desk diary she kept open near the kettle.

When Sunday finally arrived, we drove to a different café to mix things up, but the mood was awkward. On my side of the table, I was wondering if the tell-tale signs of my bloodshot eyes were giving the game away about the late night I'd just had. On Sam's side, her lack of conversation and the quiet way her head was slightly bowed with her eyes fixed on the salt and pepper shakers made me wonder if she was under some kind of sedation. She'd told me she was feeling horny just that morning in a text and I had wondered if she expected our coffee date to transition into sex back at her house. But the Sam who sat in front of me at that moment didn't seem to be the same person who'd been so enthusiastic just a few hours earlier. I didn't bother suggesting it and, instead, I just reached my hands to hold hers from across the table and then used my index finger to tilt her chin upwards, to raise her eyes towards mine.

'You seem tired, darling,' I said. 'Why don't I take you home, so you can rest and we can finish this properly another day?'

She nodded vaguely and started to get up from the table, but I still wasn't sure she understood my words. We went back to my car. I opened the door for her, then reached over her to do up her seat belt – as I'd done many times before. Her face snapped back at me with an angry look in her eyes.

'I think I can do up my own bloody seat belt!'

It was the first time she'd sounded so short with me and for a second, I was startled. It was hard to keep up. My immediate reaction was to say something back, but I stopped myself and thought for a second about what it must feel like to be an adult who prompted other people to care for you like a child, when previously she had inspired hundreds of people in her business.

When I pulled up at Sam's house, I opened the passenger door and held her hand as we walked towards the entrance. At the door, I punched the code number in, then reached my arms around her for a hug. I felt her body soften and lean into me without resistance and, as her head dropped onto my chest, I hugged her just a little bit closer, stroking the back of her head.

'Goodbye for now darling, let's talk soon to work out another date, yeah?'

She gave me a half-smile and turned away. I wondered when I'd see her again. I wondered how long we had left.

Chapter 52 – 1300 Mitch

When I couldn't see a client in real life, the solution, at times, was good old-fashioned phone sex. I don't mean old-school 0055, two-dollar-a-minute calls with badly recorded messages narrating terribly written stories about plumbers or babysitters. I mean real life, high-definition video calls, where we could sit and chat, face-to-face, and mutually masturbate if the mood felt right. Personally, I loved it. I could settle in at home, get myself all organised with my photography lights set up, hop straight out of the shower, dial in via Facetime, Skype or Zoom and get to see who I was chatting with while they could see me. During lockdown, it was a great way to bring in a few extra bucks. Many sex workers began offering the service – particularly those for whom it was a sole source of income, like me. With people unable to move around quite as freely as they once did it was the perfect solution and for my business, it was a way for new clients to test the water with someone in the sex industry without the complexities of meeting face-to-face with a stranger.

For new callers, I tended to treat it like a date. I'd sometimes have a drink in my hand and I'd encourage them to also have something to make them feel relaxed and happy. Feeling overly nervous is never a good aphrodisiac, so I'd usually start in my loungeroom for a bit of small talk and then move on to the bedroom if things progressed further. Rarely did anyone want or need a sixty-minute foreplay session on the phone though. Calls hardly ever went longer than a couple of hours and most clients were pretty happy for things to move quickly. My imagination is powerful and by letting my words paint a picture, it was fun getting the women on the other end into a mood that made them ready to touch themselves or to grab their favourite toy to lend a hand. There was something incredibly sexy about seeing a stranger getting so turned on, simply by the sound of your voice, your actions and the story you were telling them. I almost always got hard and when I watched them masturbate (and they were always very happy for me to watch), I loved seeing how excited they got and how into their bodies they became. Seeing someone bring themselves to orgasm was a lesson in efficiency, and for women who might've been looking for a quick release while working from home, or who were sneaking a quickie in while their husbands were at work, they knew exactly how to make it all run smoothly, while still having a great time.

The calls weren't always sexual, though. That is to say, the conversations usually revolved around sex, but sometimes I spoke to clients who were looking for a bit of encouragement to be bolder in their relationships or who were looking to me to help interpret something their partner (or prospective partner) did or didn't say or do. I even recall a conversation I had with a lady from Utah in the United States, who was in love with a man who was a Mormon. She was feeling a bit uneasy about his beliefs and wasn't sure how to process her feelings – or more accurately, *his* feelings about other women. I felt a little out of my depth that afternoon and there was definitely no flirting or nudity called for in that particular case. All I could do, and all I can ever do when confronted with a situation I know nothing about, is to acknowledge and listen. We ended up having an amazingly stimulating conversation, however, and I honestly believe she enjoyed it all too.

I always thought 'Virtual Mitch' would be just a small part of my business, and it was, but I really wasn't prepared for that international aspect. It just shows how relationships confuse the hell out of everyone, everywhere. Mostly though, my business remained local – or at least Australian – and the peak time for Australian women seemed to be the early evening when kids were in bed or when single women were thinking about having a relaxing drink after a long day and were looking for a bit of 'me time' to perk themselves up. It was a different thing from physical intimacy, of course, with far more talk and no hugs or gentle stroking possible to get my clients in the mood. All I could do was speak confidently and seductively, and create an environment for them to open up.

And open up they did. Once I saw the effect my words were having, and how they began touching themselves, it got me even more worked up, so the vibe I was giving off – of being totally turned on – was completely real and I was happy to show them the proof. The awkward part, I always thought, was the goodbye. I knew you couldn't just hang up straight after mutual orgasms, but the farewells were generally pretty quick because we both knew we'd achieved what we'd set out to do and there wasn't much more to say.

Many phone sex clients ended up booking me in the flesh and by the time I finally met them, knowing how to pleasure them was that little bit easier. We'd already shared a certain level of intimacy and discussed the exact things that turned each other on, so it saved a lot of guessing. When you analyse it, of course, sex is all about nerve endings and sensations, and without someone's body there in front of you, it's still possible for both parties to construct a very sexy, albeit imaginary, scene that you can finish off with real orgasms. It obviously never felt as good as physical touch with a real person, but as an add-on, I was into it and setting time aside for the odd caller who loved it just as much was becoming an important part of my working week.

It also gave me a sense of 'working' while the whole city was in lockdown, so it was good for my mental health as well.

Another interesting 'Virtual Mitch' client who comes to mind didn't feel comfortable appearing on video, or even sending me a photo for that matter, so I had to adapt my usual delivery to accommodate the lack of any sort of visuals from her end. She wanted to see me, though. Sometimes still shots in between phone calls and sometimes even quick videos. I felt like I was in *Mission Impossible* – where a disembodied voice would issue me with instructions before I embarked on a task to get that same disembodied voice to the point of orgasm.

I knew that she was from western Sydney, that she was forty-four and that she worked in healthcare. She said her name was Susan, but I didn't believe that for a second. She was always super polite and respectful towards me and her playfully youthful voice was made all the more adorable when she giggled – which she did quite often. We got on well and my initial curiosity, which bordered on frustration at times, soon became less of an issue as we got to know each other.

It was easy to feel kind of foolish when you knew someone was watching you whilst being unable to see them. It was an unequal distribution of power and it was awkward initially, but it helped pay a few bills. The other weird aspect to it was that there was never any set booking time. She'd text when she said she was horny and I'd have to make a snap decision about whether or not I could call her back – usually within the hour. If I did, we would launch almost immediately into it. Hardly any build-up and with minimal mood-setting – just her taking a chance and me having to be almost instantaneously on my game. Our conversations were always fairly quick, which was great because I got a fixed fee for the hour, and she always seemed to be satisfied. It was clear to me that she was a very sexual woman and I suspected that I was an add-on to her usual masturbatory habits and that, after working on herself for a while, she slotted in a quick conversation with me to help tip her over the edge. I loved that notion.

The thought of having this mysterious woman requesting me to call her at any time of the evening, and expecting me to perform while on the phone to her, appealed to me in another way, as well – I viewed it as a good measure of my ability to perform on the spot, under pressure, using only my mind – which had to be a good skill for an escort to have, right?

On one particular day, I remember that I was excellent – if I do say so myself. I'd had a good sleep and was in a great mood, which definitely helped with my libido. She was super horny – as usual – so I focused on thoughts of an old girlfriend I'd recently reconnected with and got erect within seconds. I then cheekily panned the camera down to show her how turned on I was. My voice was my most important tool though, and as I described to her all the things I'd theoretically like to do to her while simultaneously bringing myself to climax, I often heard her drop her phone before finishing herself off. Even if I wasn't one hundred per cent in the mood, I've always thought that the sound of a woman coming was one of the most beautiful sounds I could ever hear.

But then as soon as it all began, it would end with the usual:

'Oh my God – thank you so much, Mitch. Let's do it again soon.'

Who on Earth was this mysterious 'Susan' and what did she look like? I'd do anything to know, but I realise I probably never will.

Chapter 53 – Shopping With Sam

I'd just finished eating dinner when the first text pinged my phone. It was around 8.30 pm and Sam was asking if she could see me that night. As soon as possible. I didn't reply because it was too late and I didn't want to, but then the second text came and, a few minutes later, a third then a fourth. After a few more minutes, a fifth arrived. I made the decision not to answer any of them. I decided to text her later to tell her that I was out and that I'd only just seen her messages, but her obvious confusion in forgetting that she was contacting me so many times made me hesitant to even start the conversation. It only took a few minutes before I felt bad for ignoring her, so I shot back a reply:

Sorry, darling. I'm at dinner and just saw your message. Would you mind if I called you tomorrow?

And put my phone on silent.

Her memory was slipping faster than I thought and I became concerned about the ethics of even continuing to have bookings with a woman who was becoming so befuddled with regular life. I was starting to worry about how she could make informed consent about matters relating to her own body when her short-term memory was becoming so affected. It was a thought that had been bugging me since the whole relationship began, to be honest. I made a mental note to talk to her sister about it. I also remembered that Sam often became more confused in the evenings and that she simply had some days that were harder for her than others – so maybe that night's confusion was a combination of both.

Suddenly, the tiredness hit me. It'd been a big week. And because there weren't any mood-altering substances in the house, it was clear I was in for an uncharacteristically quiet night. I sensed that my body needed a rest anyway. Like a normal person, I had a quick shower, brushed my teeth and hit the sack. I hadn't been asleep that early in what felt like weeks, but at that moment, as my thoughts about Sam pressed down on me, it felt like the best place for me and as my head hit the pillow, I felt my breathing slow and my body start to thank me. I had my boy the following night – and he always made everything feel better.

The following day, I woke up early and gave Sam a call straight away. She made no mention of the messages the previous night, as though it had never happened. So, I just played along. We had a tiny bit of small talk before she told me she wanted to go vibrator shopping. That morning if possible. Nothing surprised me anymore and I was feeling clearheaded so I figured, why not? After clearing it with all the powers that be, in accordance with the protocol, we decided to start with a walk, during which she pointed out where her wedding took place with an edge to her voice that barely concealed her resentment. Divorce is hard at any time, but for Sam, the wound was much deeper. Her husband had a new girlfriend, and soon that girlfriend would be living full-time as a mother to Sam's children. It was a reality Sam was painfully aware of. I didn't get the sense that Sam wanted to talk about it, though. We'd spoken about it many times in the past but since her genetic test results, her thoughts had become preoccupied with her fears about that terrible and highly likely outcome. In the scheme of things, the thought of someone else raising your children was nowhere near as awful as the prospect of your disease affecting those same children.

We arrived back at her place after quite a long walk and I drove her to a nearby adult store where we laughed at some of the more ridiculous toys and tried to make things fun for a while. She had her allowance to spend and she wanted something we could use together. I recognised one of the staff members there who was incredibly knowledgeable about almost everything from anal lube to cattle prods. She valued my feedback as well. My toys were sometimes requested and I'd spent a fair bit of time looking at how well they performed and how willing people were to use them, so I usually reported all this back to the sales assistant whenever I popped in. After probably half an hour of touching, feeling and giggling, Sam picked out a very classy-looking purple and gold vibrator before we decided to head straight back to her house to try it out.

In the bedroom, I noticed that Sam had packed away the photos of herself that she previously had on her dresser. I thought about how depressing it would be to look back on your younger self being active and full of life, and I decided that I'd probably want to get rid of the photos, too. She emerged from the bathroom and I helped her undress, then slid her legs along the mattress until my tongue met her underwear. The vibrator already had some charge luckily and I flicked my thumb across the controls and watched the head of it pulse as I moved it between her legs. She giggled like a kid and I watched her body relax into the bedding as she gave in to the feeling. I used my tongue as well and got her there within minutes. And then, almost as quickly, she was ready again.

'I'm so horny.'

There was no sexiness in the way she said it. Just a statement of how she felt. I turned it on again and pushed it back between her legs as she shuddered against it. It made me so incredibly happy to still be able to do something to give her some moments of pleasure. Almost everyone deserves to feel loved – and especially my beautiful Sam.

Chapter 54 – Spinning Plates

I looked forward to seeing Sally but, at the same time, my anxiety sometimes overwhelmed me. Mitch was often an exhausting part to play and as more regulars got to know the real Dan underneath, for some reason, the more pressure I felt to perform. Because I'd revealed the chinks in my armour, it felt like I had to work harder to prove to them how good I was at hiding those chinks on demand. And Sally could be very demanding. Her need for constant touch and reassurance in my presence was tiring. Just because my hand stopped caressing her for a moment, it didn't mean I didn't find her attractive or that I wasn't horny for her. My hand was often just really sore and needed a rest. She'd made it no secret that she was particularly smitten with me and because she had the funds to pay for my time, her regular bookings had become an important contribution to my income. I was aware that that could potentially get tricky down the track. The more I sensed her jealousy about who I was with and what I might be saying or doing to them during my bookings, the more I realised her emotions were becoming very real, and that the already blurred boundaries were becoming almost non-existent.

Sexually speaking, Sally pushed me to higher and higher levels every time we were together. I knew her body intimately and the double-edged sword of that was that I had to combine the knowledge with an explorer's passion to keep providing her with something new each time. I sometimes wondered how many different ways you could really have sex. I was convinced we'd tried pretty much all of them – and we were now honing our skills into a fine art.

Not that there was anything wrong with repeat performances of something brilliant to begin with. The tried-and-true methods are often the best, and if something consistently works, why change it? What was amazing about my sexual connection with Sally was that, no matter how exhausted her sexual requests made me feel, she had this fantastic way of knowing exactly how to push my body further and further – and she always got my body to respond to her needs, no matter how worn out I thought I was.

Each time I was preparing to go to her place or the hotel room she had booked, the anxiety started again. Could we recreate that same energy another time? But there was something that seemed to make it impossible to fail. When we were together, there were fireworks, and every time I closed the door after saying goodbye, I would once again float home, filled with that same wonderful sense of inner peace.

Chapter 55 – Managing Mum

My parents never asked me about my work and, although it didn't really surprise me, I still felt disappointed in a way that's hard to articulate.

One morning, after I'd dropped my son at school, I popped in to visit them before heading off to the gym. As Mum slid a cup of coffee towards me from across the table, I wanted her to ask about more than how my son was going at school, what I thought of the pandemic management or whether or not I looked like I'd gained weight since she last saw me. Just once, I wanted to chat about other things, and with Mum especially, I felt like I had so much more I wanted to let her know.

As a woman, I was sure her idea of what I did for a living was tainted with sordid details. I imagined that, despite the unconditional love she had for me as her son, there was a chunk of her that saw me as a bit of a slacker who had contrived a hare-brained scheme to work as a male escort just so I could sleep in and avoid the real world. But she would be wrong. Well, maybe she was right about the sleeping in and real world stuff, but even then, it was always so much more. I wanted to tell her what I'd learned about women and what it had also taught me about men. I wished I could tell her about my battle to be more patient in life and how I lay awake some nights worrying about Sam and the day when she didn't recognise her children, or me, anymore. What was worst, though, was the persistent guilt I felt about my ex and how she must've felt when I left to be a boyfriend-for-hire. All her dreams of sharing a future with me as her stable, loyal husband were ruined when I walked out in an optimistic haze with seemingly little regard for anyone but myself and my need for complete independence.

I didn't share any of this with Mum, though, as I always felt the need to justify what I'd done. I would've liked to have talked to her about all the women I saw who just wanted someone kind to listen to them. Someone to remind them that their body and soul were equally beautiful – and that they could learn to love themselves again. I had so many stories about women I'd seen who struggled with trust issues and I wanted to talk with her about the fragility of self-esteem and the impact other people could have on your own view of self-worth and respect. If anyone knew that feeling, it was me. If I thought too long about what my mum thought about me, I'd fill with the dull ache of shame I'd begun to think I deserved. I never used to feel such shame, but since I'd come out about it, I'd begun to feel it more than ever and I really needed their help to feel like I was making a difference in other people's lives. I wondered, does this same need exist so strongly in everyone?

I grew up feeling valued and loved by my parents. They were hard-working and kind, and only ever wanted the best for me. But, still, there was a lingering emptiness that I was never able to come to terms with. I wondered if Mum had told any of her friends what I did and suspected that, if she had, it was accompanied by a wringing of her hands and a plea for some sensible advice about how on Earth she was going to convince me to change my ways.

There were things I wanted to tell Dad, too. His take on things, I thought, would be different, but maybe he had that same sense of shame in my choices because he saw me as someone's toy – a guy who does things he doesn't really want to do, with clients who don't respect him or treat him with any sort of pride. And that's pretty much how sex workers come across in the movies. We're either extremely damaged goods whose early lives had been marred by abuse and neglect, or we're manipulative hustlers who might have come from the wrong side of the tracks originally, but were now just trying to do whatever we could to exit the industry. I was neither of those things. And even with my occasional binges (okay, *frequent* binges) and the fact that I usually drank every single day – alone – I honestly didn't feel like the sad case I suspected my parents thought I was. I made an effort to be a good son to them. I tried to visit (or at least call) regularly, I helped around the house, helped them with their technological struggles and I showed them how much I loved *my* son and how I treated the women in my life with kindness and respect.

I knew that, more than anything, I wasn't a bad guy. And I wouldn't let anyone treat me as such. I knew they thought that as well, but I did wonder what they really thought – deep down – as hard as that might've been to hear. Generally, whenever I told someone about what I did, especially when it came to older people, I found they quickly moved the discussion along. I'm not sure whether this was because they felt uncomfortable or whether it was because they had so many questions, they didn't know where to start. As a result, I quickly became very good at sizing up the person I was talking to, and deciding whether I was going to be a photographer or an escort – should the inevitable question be asked.

I wanted my parents to know that I really was in the business of helping people and hopefully enriching their lives and in return, they were giving me purpose and a feeling of worth as well. Sure, I'd been gifted expensive watches, beautiful jewellery and amazing clothes, but it was also the loving messages and kindness shown to me that kept me going. My heart swells even thinking of them now. My parent's discomfort was palpable, though, and my revelation, and the way it spread within certain branches of my family tree, made extended family gatherings very awkward at times. I was sure my parents preferred that nobody else knew and, possibly, if they were completely honest, I think they might have preferred not to know themselves. It had to be done, though. I saw the cogs turning in my dad's head – especially with the overseas trips and the way I always seemed to be home during the day, but out at night. I worried that they might have thought I was a drug dealer. *No, Mum and Dad*, I thought, *it's okay – everything I do is legal.*

Well, sort of...

Chapter 56 – The Turning Point

It was another Saturday night in Melbourne and I was alone. My Adelaide tour was over and Sydney was two weeks away. The booking a new client made with me a while ago had fallen through and there was no interest from anyone else at the time.

I had a fair bit of coke on me, so I lined it up with a vodka and tonic and told myself I was allowed to have a good time. By the time I'd had my second line, I was feeling restless and my finger flicked on the TV remote and, what do you know? *The Notebook* was on. It was the scene where the wife momentarily no longer recognised her husband and screamed at him to get away from her as if he was some stranger and she was in danger. I knew it was just a movie, but my mind was never far from Sam and I wondered where she was at that moment. I wondered if she was also afraid. It had been a while since our last catch-up, so when I sent her a text, I kept it light and breezy so as not to appear like some kind of stalker.

Speaking of stalkers, my gay client from Adelaide wouldn't stop messaging me. I even received a text from her phone number, but from a different person claiming to be her wife, telling me to never contact 'her woman' again. I ignored and blocked it. My message to Sam was far more friendly.

Hi, hun! I just wanted to see how you are...

She replied straight away.

Missing you.

If we kept texting, she might've asked me to come over right then, but with the last line of coke still dripping down the back of my throat, I knew that it would be pointless for me and not fair on her. All I needed was to hear from her, to know she was safe. I wrote back again in emojis, blowing her a kiss and inviting her to set a date with me soon so she didn't have to miss me for much longer.

I will, she wrote back.

I reached for the remote and turned the TV off, then picked up my phone to text Sally to tell her that I'd been thinking about her. It was the booze talking. But even before my finger pressed the first key, I felt like a cheating boyfriend and changed my mind. I only just texted Sam. I couldn't text Sally straight after. But yes, I could actually. Of *course* I could. It was part of the job. I was an escort by profession and because I didn't do much else, I found the line between work and life had been obscured for a long time. I wondered if it was ever clear, for that matter. Life was lonely, even when the work was there, but when it temporarily dried up, the isolation became almost unbearable. Fortunately, my recent acquisition of a half-ounce of coke would see me through the week so, given I'd taken it pretty easy the night before, I thought it might be fun to have a bit of a party by myself. It was a beautiful, clear night so I thought it might also be nice to have a strum of the guitar on my balcony. I knew I wouldn't sleep that night anyway, so my next text was to my awesome friend whose company I always appreciated at times like this.

I'm in a booking, she wrote back. *I'll text you after.*

I loved it when my friends replied in the middle of bookings. I found it kind of hot.

I didn't feel like being alone that night, so I poured myself another drink, lined up another fat, white slug and picked up the guitar. I knew I couldn't keep doing this forever, but I really didn't give a shit at that point...

***

The next afternoon, I woke up feeling like a complete idiot. The reality kicked in when I noticed the bright red blood on my singlet and then I remembered. I did that. I completely lost my shit. The evidence was on my phone as well. My heart was racing as I scrolled through the messages that I'd sent to various people and I felt like crawling back under my doona, never to face the world again.

It wasn't just one thing that set me off. I think it was the lack of work, combined with my solitude, that gave me too much time to think and my worsening self-hatred had been amplified as a result. It was virtually impossible to stay upbeat. I knew I could be living an easier life. I knew I *could* be earning good money as a qualified lawyer who left the house at a set time each morning with my little briefcase and my packed lunch, and in my shiny, late model car. I *could* be coming home in time for dinner with my wife and son and paying off a mortgage quickly. I *could* enjoy conversations with my parents about the hearings I'd worked on that day, and I *could* even feel what it's like to have your own family not think of you as an out-of-control nutcase – but I didn't make those choices. The need I had to be different never left me and, even though I thought the career change might've made that desire go away, the truth was that, in many ways, they'd only become intensified. In the good moments, I felt better than ever before. That particular morning was not one of those moments.

I'd had way too much coke, for starters. In fact, I'd had too much of everything that night. I even remembered throwing some ketamine into the mix and as a result, decided it would be a good idea to do a bit of marketing by 'flirting' with a few regulars who hadn't booked me for a while. But as the coke, booze, ket and weed kicked in and loosened my tongue, my approach became too cocky, too quickly. The boundary between the Mitch I had created and the Dan I really was came crashing down only to let everybody see the tangled mess of my life and how I didn't seem to have a fucking clue what I was doing. I found myself telling a wealthy client about my lockdown-related money woes. I was obviously grifting and when she saw through my thinly-veiled attempts at self-pity, she asked about my intentions straight out:

Do you need some money?

I was just as open in return.

I do. Can you help me?

She transferred a small amount into my account while we were still chatting via text. She said it was because she felt worried about me and just wanted to make sure I was looking after myself. She also told me that she could tell I was on something and that worried her even more.

I'd given away far too much of myself that night. So, that following afternoon, I woke up with someone else's money sitting in my bank account. All thanks to a generous woman who I hadn't seen in ages and someone I'd probably blown any chance of seeing again professionally. I must have looked like a cliché to her – the drug-addled hopeless prostitute who couldn't even pay the rent on his crappy apartment in St Kilda. I broke my rules and sent Sam a text as well, but she didn't reply. I then sat there feeling emotional, stressed and alone, wondering if maybe she was already non compos mentis and had forgotten who I was or, something that felt even worse to me – that she still remembered me but just wasn't interested anymore.

And that's probably when I pulled apart that disposable razor. I've already mentioned that I used to cut myself when I was younger, just to see how painful it would be. Unfortunately, in my messed-up mind, it felt good. Back then, I was convinced that a bit of pain was a good thing and the previous night that old feeling had come back.

But what I did next made it even worse.

After running the blade across my chest and watching the droplets of blood spring to the surface of my skin, I took a selfie and sent it to the long-suffering sex worker friend I'd contacted the night before – before I lost all control. When I re-read the incoherent message that accompanied the picture, it came across almost as a completely self-indulgent, cruel and twisted taunt.

I'm a FKIN who're,. I wannto fuckn die.

It was truly disgusting behaviour.

Drugs make you so incredibly self-absorbed, it's simply revolting.

Repugnant.

I was projecting my self-hatred onto her with clearly no concern for how she would react and I put her in an awful position.

I'm so glad I didn't get a response.

I was surprised that she even spoke to me again after that, but she did forgive me. She knew what I was like and she's one of the most non-judgmental people I have ever met – a truly wonderful woman and an excellent professional companion. Her graciousness made me feel even worse, though. She'd had a tough life, too. What I did with that bloody-chested selfie was an exercise in textbook manipulation and I never want to be that way again. I felt as close to being suicidal as I'd felt in a long, long time but the fact that I didn't take it any further told me that I still had a rational mind hidden away, somewhere...

I never wanted to cause pain to other people by killing myself. I didn't want my son going through life wondering why his dad didn't love him enough to stick around and I didn't want to make anybody who encountered me feel a millisecond of guilt that maybe they missed a signal or two, and that they could have done something to stop me.

After a while, I sobered up a bit, and messaged my friend.

I'm so, so sorry.

She immediately wrote back.

X.

Chapter 57 – A Scare

Sam used to love it when I hugged her after sex, but on that occasion, just as our breathing was slowing after another forced and fairly mediocre session in bed, I noticed the shift. My arms were wrapped around her when she suddenly pulled away for a moment and looked at me with a flash of fear. It was fast, but noticeable. *Oh shit,* I thought, *did she forget?*

I quickly reminded her how good the sex was when we experimented with sensory play that one time a while ago, to see if I could jog a memory, and make her realise that she was safe and that we'd been together before. Fortunately, she came back just as quickly. The feeling was fleeting, but it unnerved the hell out of me. I held her for a bit longer, then mentioned that I needed to start getting ready to go. She looked really tired and told me she wanted to stay in bed, so I gently kissed her again, tucked her in and said goodbye. She nodded and closed her eyes, so I took that as my cue to leave, making sure the door was securely locked as I stepped out into the street.

I had another booking the next afternoon and I needed to get home to shower and rest. I would be washing the taste and scent of Sam off my skin, but the vision of her laying there, bundled up in her bedding, looking so small and alone, was much harder to remove.

Chapter 58 –
Locked Down and Locked Out

Now I was feeling truly alone. The pandemic wasn't going away anytime soon and life in Melbourne had become a revolving door of lockdowns, with enforced curfews and travel restrictions. Yes, you could technically leave home to spend the night with a significant other as long as they lived within five kilometres of you – but using that as an excuse to work seemed too risky. I developed a growing anxiety that each new message from a possible client asking if I would break curfew to come and visit them was actually the cops trying to bust sex workers like me.

All over the city, people were more in need of human touch and companionship than ever before but, instead, they had to endure isolation. For me, that meant no income. I began to resent the freedom my clients in other states had and am sure many of them saw other, more available companions which just made my feeling of redundance worse. For Sam's carers, it meant a heightened panic to add to their long list of ongoing worries about her daily care, so the decision was made that I should stop seeing her. Although I could have run a good argument that I was a caregiver and could maybe see her without a penalty, the possibility of spreading the virus to an already health-compromised client was far too risky to contemplate.

The rest of my clients missed me too, but with the option of contacting me via phone, text, or video, I was offering them some sort of a service at least, and this also helped me out a bit financially. It wasn't the same, though. It was definitely not the same money and for Sam, it was pretty much pointless. Her memory was still fading and as it slipped, so too did her ability to focus on me when all I could be to her was a disembodied voice on the other end of the phone. The more frequent each lockdown became, the more I would wonder about whether I would even see her again and if she'd remember who I was if I eventually did. We exchanged a couple of texts, but she sent me back replies that became more and more brief. Only single word replies to acknowledge my own conversation without discussing anything further. I decided I should wait to see if she thought of texting me without my prompting. And then I would wait some more... COVID continued to keep us prisoner and I wondered when it would all end. Or if.

When Sam's texts finally did arrive, they were usually short messages to tell me she'd been missing me, but the conversation petered out after just a couple of lines. It felt like the beginning of the end, and I wasn't sure how to process it. On the one hand, being with her had become incredibly challenging and just a little bit less sexy each time. On the other hand, however, I felt myself already beginning to mourn her. I loved her dearly but was always conscious of the need to fortify my heart, given the inevitability of our situation. Perhaps the legally enforced boundaries we had to abide by were a small blessing in disguise...

Chapter 59 –
The Beginning of the End

Once the gruelling, seemingly never-ending lockdown eventually lifted, Sam said she wanted to see me more often, but it was well and truly out of her hands by then. For some reason, Sam told her friend about the mix-up when I was in Queensland all those months ago and about how she stood on my street corner and couldn't get in – and the friend was understandably so shocked, she proceeded to put in place a new, more controlled plan. A plan where each date was determined well in advance, set in stone and transport would be pre-arranged. Sam was frustrated at the loss of control, which seemed all about confining her libido to locked-in times and dates.

'But what if I'm horny on a different day?' she once said. It was a reasonable concern, I thought.

My reaction was a mixture of sharing her frustration and offering her a sympathetic ear on one hand and feeling happy that, maybe, I had one less thing to worry about, now – there would be no more confused calls and texts, and no more bookings that were cancelled or forgotten.

One night, I stupidly revealed to her that I liked coke. After all the confessions she seemed to like making to her friends, I was petrified that she would broadcast *that* to everyone as well. Reassuringly, though, she didn't. All she wanted was to try it herself. She wanted to experience *everything* before she died, she said. I told her I'd see what I could do but that was rubbish. I thought back to the dressing-down I got when her friend thought I wasn't using condoms during our bookings and of course, I knew that I would never, ever, provide Sam with drugs. And I certainly didn't need my legal experience to tell me how incredibly negligent I would be if anything went wrong. Besides, her poor brain had more than enough to cope with, without adding substance abuse to the list. At our next official booking, she didn't mention it again and I was glad.

On our first date under the new system, we had a nice dinner together at my apartment, thanks to the convenience of Uber Eats. I was just about to start tidying up when I heard Sam call out from my bedroom. She wanted to fuck and she wanted to fuck NOW. I tried to accommodate her but I wasn't in the mood at all. At one point, I called for a time out to compose myself in the bathroom and after a couple of minutes, I could hear her singing, 'Whyyy are we waiiiiting?' She was really pissed off that my desires didn't match hers and, no matter how hard I tried, I couldn't get hard.

I worried that I shouldn't have eaten so much but thought that the real reason for my lack of enthusiasm may have something to do with my recent binges combined with how familiar and predictable our lovemaking had become. Also, and this was something I didn't want to admit to anyone, including myself, I'd noticed that she'd forgone her usual shower and maintenance routine before seeing me this time, which had the potential to become a further niggling issue I had to deal with. Nevertheless, Sam was seriously pissed off with me. She claimed my erection issue had happened before – but it honestly hadn't – not once. But who was I to argue with a woman who had a failing memory?

I felt extremely hurt, refunded her some money and dropped her home early that night. I was devastated. Teary, in fact. Our reunion had been a complete mess. She texted me at 11 pm, telling me not to beat myself up about it, but my mood had already shifted irrevocably. So I just completely ignored her. My pride was shot and I was down a substantial amount of money that I really, really needed.

I made a snap decision to cancel my upcoming Adelaide tour, refunded the deposits from the few people who had already booked me and, as I paced around my living room, I told myself that I'd had enough of it all – and I meant it. I thought that maybe things would seem different in the light of day, so I messaged my dealer. I was down a few hundred bucks on where I should have been, so what was another grand in the scheme of things? It seemed like money well spent if it was going to lift my spirits and help me forget the slump I was in and how hard things were becoming. It seemed like a sensible enough knee-jerk reaction, so I ran with it, and when my phone buzzed about thirty minutes later, I threw a shirt on – ignoring the staggered wounds across my chest – and stomped downstairs in my bare feet to collect the blow he brought me, hidden in an empty pack of cigarettes. My head turned away from the security cameras that monitored the foyer as I slipped him the cash.

'Cheers for the smokes, mate.'

I then headed back upstairs and proceeded to completely write myself off.

Again.

Chapter 60 – Silence

It was strange. As the weeks passed, I found myself missing Sam more than ever; at times, it felt like I cared for her almost as much as I did my own son. But I also found myself in a constant struggle between trying to be my usual, fairly optimistic self, while also resigning myself to the fact that there was nothing I could do to save her. Lots of things made me think of her and it happened in the most unexpected moments. It could've been when I was watching TV, or maybe doom-scrolling the news online, and something about Alzheimer's might pop up. Occasionally, I'd stop what I was doing and either turn the volume up or I'd click a link – craving for any good news. At other times, I'd just ignore it all and pretend I wasn't interested. I couldn't see the point anyway. I knew I couldn't make a difference. Not for Sam, anyway.

It had been ages since our last attempt at sex and the new system we'd put in place had gone out the window. I thought about everything that had happened that last time we were together and I wondered once again if that was going to be our final goodbye. I couldn't bear the thought. That last time we saw each other, I noticed the way that she was more embarrassed than usual about the mistakes she thought she made with me too. She didn't like realising she'd forgotten something important or that she behaved in a way she shouldn't have and I wished that I could have had one more chance to tell her that none of that mattered. I could see that the control her carers had over her, to keep her safe, was becoming increasingly difficult for her to deal with, but I also knew she accepted that there was no other practical solution. That was her life, now.

I couldn't begin to imagine what living that life must be like, and the times when those thoughts crept in always left me feeling unsettled, empty and sad. I used to think of her on the days I had my son, in those moments when he would come running up to me in the schoolyard, with his arms outstretched, so happy to be with me again after a long day at school. How would I feel if he knew our time was limited and eventually he'd never see me again? How could he possibly process why Daddy wasn't there anymore? It just tore me apart thinking about what her kids must be going through and how much harder it would become for them. I wondered if I'd ever feel like doing normal things again if I was in Sam's position. Could I eat, or sleep, or even get out of bed? I doubted it. Would I even want to bother? Probably not.

Sam made a joke once about having a few male escorts as her pallbearers but it was just so incredibly sad to me, and obvious to both of us, that she was trying to use humour to handle thoughts about the end of her life. Yes, she had the worries of wondering what it would feel like to miss out on her children growing up, but she also had to absorb the reality that her slide into complete memory loss would also slowly erase her presence from the world, even while she was still alive. Eventually, she'd remember nothing – not even herself – and as the people who loved her dealt with the confronting truth of that terrible demise, they'd also start to forget who she used to be as well.

Separating from her husband must have made it harder. Already, another woman was completely immersed in the lives of her children and, while that's something so many divorced couples go through, in Sam's case, she had the added indignity of being forced to withdraw from the task of motherhood against her will – prematurely and whilst she could still make a difference. She was painfully aware that so much of her children's lives would be guided and supported by a woman she barely knew and wouldn't ever really get to know – and there would be nothing to be gained by casting this new woman as some sort of evil stepmother. She would be, Sam knew, the woman they would need to feel happily connected to. It was such a bloody awful disease.

I wanted to call her many times, but I stopped myself. It was partly because I was scared that I might've been seen to be putting pressure on her, at a time when she was vulnerable. Having been connected to her life as her provider and companion – the man who exchanged his time for her money – I imagined that many of the people in her life might see me as an opportunist trying to scratch out another few dollars before she completely lost her mind. But then, there was the struggle I had with myself. I came into this industry to create a business, with an aim to make money, build a client list and create a lifestyle where I could finally feel like myself. When I first listed Mitch Larsson in that directory, I didn't imagine that anyone like Sam would come into my life. Someone who would force me to think so deeply about my own responses to life, love and loss. I didn't think that being a sex worker would throw my inadequacies and failings up in front of me in such a dramatic, unforgiving way. I wanted to know if Sam was safe but, on a selfish level, I wanted to make sure that I hadn't let her down. That's the last thing I ever wanted to do. Dealing with her made me understand patience in new ways, but I still had so much more to learn. I decided to practice that patience by giving it another week before I gave into my fear by just contacting her anyway. I had to know where I stood.

Sally texted me to schedule our next booking and, just as I managed to quash my fears for Sam, the anxiety about whether I could fulfil Sally's desires distracted me from my thoughts and began a whole new kind of churning in my gut. When I thought about Sam, I worried about not being enough, and when I thought about Sally, that same fear consumed me. It was becoming a recurring theme.

My confidence was fading, my mojo was lost and I didn't think I was good enough for anyone.

And I wondered if I ever could be again.

Chapter 61 –
The Prospect of Love

I suppose everything must come to an end at some point. Sometimes, it's quick and clean and happens as you expect it to. Other times, things limp slowly to the finish line and you realise it should have stopped a long time ago. With Sam, I knew it would definitely end, and that when it did, it would be quite sudden – and very final. I wasn't sure how Sally and I would end, though. If I measured it by the passion of our lovemaking, I thought it could be in some sort of fiery explosion – with someone's heart getting broken. Would it be mine? Hers? Or both?

Familiarity might breed a kind of contempt, but it also builds a type of love and longing that happens when you know someone is there for you and you like the way that steadiness feels. I was the type of guy who found predictability boring, however, and even though every single time I met Sally it became a wild adventure in boundary-pushing and limitation testing, even that knowledge brought its own unique kind of boredom. I wondered what the hell was wrong with me? I'd formed the most amazing connections with incredibly inspiring women that other men would love to have met, but I was still out there, like some attention-starved only child, always looking for something more.

She'd booked me again for our regular catch-up and I was the usual swirling mess of delight mixed with dysfunction. The sex would be great, I knew. She'd make me feel good about myself because she wanted me so badly. But in the same breath, she had the power to make me feel completely inadequate because I worried that I couldn't possibly keep up with the satisfaction she craved. The job brought me close to people in spectacularly intimate, yet incredibly isolating ways. Mitch the ladies' man rode out into the wide world in Ubers, but Dan, the insecure addict, would always come home alone, and Sally made me feel that more than almost anyone I was with. Yes, she said she wanted me, and part of me even felt like she had already fallen in love with me, but the 'me' she wanted wasn't entirely real, and if we were to explore a life together, I knew I'd disappoint her eventually.

I knew she'd set a cracking pace so, as usual, I made sure I slept well the night before. I brought a few toys on that occasion to give my own body a break should my stamina fade. And I didn't mean just the physical exertion. Being so incredibly desirous of touch – endless touch – did more than make my hands and body ache. It made that fractured heart of mine ache, too. Sometimes, I wondered what it was about her that needed to receive so much attention. Then there were the other times when I wondered what it was about me she liked and should I even question her craving me. Having experienced crippling loneliness, insecurity, and an overwhelming need for human touch many, many times throughout my life did give me a pretty good understanding of where she was coming from, though.

I knew I couldn't be Mitch forever, as much as I liked to imagine seeing the rest of my forties out in this wonderful world of love, kindness and compassion. Deep down, I was sure Sally wouldn't be there forever, either. She was a stunning woman who was great company and, although I worried that she might have fallen for the wrong person, the fun we had in each other's company was hard to resist when it was so willingly on offer. I'd been questioning whether I was a relationship kind of guy, but my need to be loved and appreciated reassured me that there was a chance I was.

Things needed to change, though.

I needed to change.

Finding love as a sex worker isn't an easy thing to do, and I always assumed it would never happen as long as I was in the industry. I couldn't possibly expect someone to share their heart with me, while I shared mine with so many others. I also thought that, for some of my regular clients, finding love in their own lives while still tethered to me emotionally wouldn't be easy, either.

I'd left Sally's that night, slightly dizzy from yet another wild romp together. I didn't think it was possible, but she'd pushed me harder than ever before – not only physically this time but emotionally as well. We'd dabbled in a little MDMA, which heightened our emotions significantly. At one point, we were both sobbing after an incredibly intense conversation about the reality of our relationship, which led to some of the most mind-blowingly sensual sex we'd ever had. It felt like we'd both finally had a chance to share our concerns and fears, realised we felt exactly the same way, and consequently made love like it was our first and last time.

By the time I arrived home, I barely had the energy to suck down a quick drink before I collapsed into a much-needed, long and deep sleep.

Chapter 62 – Burning Out

After I'd seen Sally, it felt like I'd taken the world's most effective anti-depressant. In the days that followed, I felt like my life had meaning. Colours appeared to be more vibrant, I sang a lot and I generally felt back on track. I'd look forward to hearing from her because she always wanted to secure our next date as early as possible and that meant more happiness. On those occasions, it was easy to tell what triggered my 'highs'.

The 'lows' were different, though. Usually, without warning, I'd find myself waking up and immediately wondering what on Earth I was waking up for, and I'd generally be a grumpy prick for most of the week, wondering when the next high would come to save me. Dealing with bipolar was kind of like walking around with a live hand grenade in your pocket. You thought you'd worked your way through every module of the basic training you need to know to be a functioning adult, but then your guard would slip and you'd become complacent and push life that little bit harder because you'd convinced yourself that you were okay before realising, too late, that you actually weren't. And then it would happen all over again. Every four to six weeks. Year after year. Almost like clockwork.

I was a very emotional guy who had chosen to completely immerse himself in a world that screamed at me with a whole spectrum of emotions and when I stopped and thought about it, it made sense – of course it would affect me. The emptiness I felt in between the growing number of bookings I had with strangers and regulars was obviously going to take its toll. But then, I'd think, how could I feel alone when I was fortunate enough to be cared for by so many wonderful people? I'd left my marriage because I craved independence, and because my heart felt too big for just one woman. Yet, there I was – living a life that would form lots of men's ultimate fantasies but somehow remaining hollow and unfulfilled.

The need I had for 'normal person' conversation hadn't gone away, either. On the rare occasion I'd visit Mum and Dad, they never asked me how work was and they usually just wanted reassurance that I was staying afloat financially. I got mad at myself for even feeling disappointed about their lack of interest because, honestly, did I *really* expect that I could drag them into this strange, unknown world and they'd just wholeheartedly embrace everything they saw? In my heart, I wished that they could talk to me about what I did without casting any judgement or without feeling like they'd failed. In my more rational moments, though, I understood that my actions had dismantled an entire lifetime of their hopes and dreams – and really tested their faith in the decisions I'd made. Coming to terms with that kind of stuff doesn't happen overnight. My mind would flash forward to my own son's adulthood and I'd think about the things he could tell me about himself that might've caused that same level of parental disappointment. If I was honest with myself, as much as I would try to help him live a life free from the weight of my own expectations of him, there was another part of me that understood exactly how my parents felt. Acknowledging that truth gave me clarity, but it was only the beginning. I had no idea what the relationship I had with my parents would end up looking like, but I had to believe that it would only get better and return to normal. I didn't always make the best choices, but they were *my* choices and I hoped that if I ever needed to ask for help, they would be there for me. I'd always been a fairly proud and stubborn bastard, though, so the odds were that the moment would never come to pass.

I wasn't ready for rehab just yet, but the fact that the regular calls to my dealer hadn't stopped, and the sales staff at my local bottle shop knew me by name, had to be a sign that it was time to slow down. It was good that I hadn't Googled medical advice about panic attacks and drug overdoses in ages, but on the negative side, it was probably only because I'd become used to living in a world of disorder and unpredictability. Would I actually ever make it to rehab? And what would happen to me if I didn't? It was a big question, but the even bigger question was – what would happen to Mitch if I did?

My mental health issues weren't fun, but they were mine. If I fixed them, would it mean also saying goodbye to my spontaneity, my various schemes, my grandiose plans, and my dreams? In my darker days, it was those dreams that kept me going and managed to throw an optimistic beacon of light towards my future. They made me feel as though I had something to head towards, even though, like a moth banging itself against a lightbulb, I wasn't sure what I was supposed to do when I got there. My mood hadn't reached its lowest ebb yet, but the black dog was never far away. I kept telling myself that I was winning but when the partying stopped and the headaches remained, I realised the opposite could be true.

I had another tour coming up, though, and the promise of work and the prospect of earning some good money kept me going. The next stop was Sydney again, where I had some dates with a couple of regulars, as well as a first-timer – so my calendar was full. There was also an additional date I wasn't too sure about but, because it was just a quick social date, it didn't matter so much if she cancelled. The trip would still be profitable. I made a note to myself to text that client again to try to gauge her level of commitment. Understanding women was becoming something

I'd become better at, but I still had so much to learn if I was going to get any better at minimising my interactions with time-wasters. I was hoping that the trip would be the jolt I needed to get back into sexy, driven Mitch mode – all professional and one hundred per cent customer-focused.

Chapter 63 –
Finally Taking Control

I was sitting on the plane heading back home, sucking down as much pinot gris as the flight attendant would give me and in a thoroughly foul mood. Sydney wasn't the success I thought it would be at all. I went there with the promise of seeing regulars, as well as one new client to fund my journey but what I ended up with was one shit booking with a self-righteous princess and two cancellations from women I thought were a certainty.

I'd been seeing one who seemed to think I should be her exclusive property even though she'd only booked me twice, so maybe that was a blessing in disguise. I decided to cut down on the phone calls and text messages I shared with her because I was giving too much away – not just my time that should have been paid for when we chatted and giggled and flirted with each other on the phone, but too much of Dan. Many of my clients knew my real name; they knew that I was a dad and sometimes even knew my son's name. They knew all about how I'd ruined my marriage and they even knew my issues with my wellbeing, my drug habits and the self-esteem that could see me strutting around like a rock star one minute and blubbering like an inconsolable idiot the next. One client might look at me breathlessly with her own pleasure still shining on my face and declare me a God, while the next client – like that princess in Sydney – might demand a refund because, despite me busting my arse to make her come, claimed the whole experience 'wasn't as she expected'.

My whole life felt like a lie and a failure. I'd created a persona that was meant to be sexy, strong, suave and fun, but underneath it all, I was always just me – a regular guy who worried about why he couldn't be perfect every time. I felt like never touring again. When I first began touring, I dived into it like some exotic first-class business trip, which it technically often was, but as the darker times grew more frequent, I invariably felt like a rent-boy who was at the beck and call of clients who didn't always treat me with the respect I'd hoped for. Platinum status on various airlines, complimentary crap from various hotels around the world – all that meant nothing to me if a job went badly and Mitch couldn't fulfil the dreams he promised he could.

Welcome to the wonderful world of sex work.

Sometimes you're up, sometimes you're down. I never really knew many other people in the industry except for a couple of trusted friends and from them, I heard the same stories. For the girls, physical safety is more of a concern, but it's the emotional dangers we all share. People either don't care enough about you or they seem to care too much. Both scenarios can be equally dangerous in their own ways. I messaged one of those dear friends and she helped talk me down from the proverbial ledge.

'When in doubt...' she said, 'read your testimonials.'

She was right, of course. So I did. Surely I didn't fluke it all those times. But if I was going to survive, I needed to find better ways to manage myself and better ways to cope with the times that didn't go to plan. I never regretted making the leap from lawyer to full-time father to professional lover but I needed to get smarter, and I needed it to make it happen ASAP.

It all had to start with better screening. I'd always made it pretty much a condition of booking me that I would chat to the client, for free, to get an idea of what I was in for – as well as to let them know what to expect from me. Discernment can be measured in lots of ways, though. It doesn't have to be about meanness or the idea that someone's not good enough for you. It's more about looking inward and focusing on yourself. I was starting to believe that I deserved better and that, for the benefit of my mental health, as well as my potential clients, I needed to start saying 'no'. My girlfriends in the industry are shining examples of how much happier you can be if you just took it a little easier on yourself by weeding out certain clients who demanded too much without giving you much in return. I'd been in the business of building the self-esteem of countless clients who I thought deserved only the best, most respectful partners, so perhaps it was time for me to look after myself as well.

I decided to put my newfound resolve into practice a few days later when I took a call from a client who had seen me before. Every time, it had been pretty damn ordinary. It had nothing to do with shallow things, like her appearance or how she was in bed, but was more about her as a person. If she wasn't talking incessantly at me about how much of a 'goddess' she was and about how many times she'd 'saved' me and countless other male escorts, she was treating me like her whipping boy by constantly reminding me how lucky I was to be seeing her. I'd always leave our bookings feeling worthless and feeling like an imposter. I didn't want to feel like that anymore.

I knew I couldn't change the stigma of how people perceived the work I did. That stuff doesn't happen overnight, and maybe it won't ever happen, but the notion that we, as sex workers, are anything less than regular people running completely legitimate and quite complex businesses doesn't sit well with me. I could simply shrug it off as not my problem and admit that I can't control everything, but the truth is that everyone in the industry has a small, unspoken part to play in defending what we do. How we react to things when in the public eye, how professionally we conduct ourselves with clients and potential clients, as well as how we present ourselves on social media, all play a part in the overall perception of our industry. And on that day, this particular client was telling me she wanted me for an overnight booking in Adelaide but informed me that, this time, she would decide whether she'd pay me my full amount or not *after* the booking – as 'a lady's prerogative'.

My reaction was to tell her, 'I'm sorry but I'm not interested. I think it would be best if you found someone more suited to you. I'm clearly not giving you what you need anymore.'

She was not at all happy about being turned down but I told her that my decision was not up for negotiation. I wanted to be a provider in the best possible sense. I certainly didn't get into this to be anyone's whore. The power of that simple word leaving my lips gave me some kind of new spring in my step and, although my mind had a temporary vision of the bills that were waiting and the thousands of dollars I just kissed goodbye, I reminded myself that choosing this lifestyle could never be about the money. And never was. As much as I wanted to work with women who needed reminders of the people they were, and still could be, I needed to think the same of myself, too.

I'd seen that particular client quite a few times before and initially, it had been quite wonderful. She was very respectful to me, she always picked me up at the airport before taking me either to her home or to lovely hotels and she always paid upfront, with little fanfare. As our relationship deepened, she began to bad-mouth other male escorts she'd been with or started making comments suggesting she didn't 'need' us, and on a few occasions, she simply ignored me while talking for ages to her friends on the phone in my presence. I believe that as her confidence around men grew, thanks to her time with male escorts, her initial kindness turned into a sort of female chauvinism. I sensed that she was still very insecure and I honestly hoped her kindness towards me would return, but after her 'lady's prerogative' remark, I couldn't tolerate it any longer. It was a real shame, because we were once quite good friends who had been through a lot together and I still miss her to a degree, but unfortunately, she became one of the few clients I've had who I refused to see again. And I'm comfortable with that.

It felt like the Mitch Larsson 'brand' changed after that tour and after my interaction with that client. Sure, I was making a lot less money than I once was, but I became much happier as a result. I was never abrupt or cold-hearted when I declined a booking but if it didn't feel one hundred per cent right to me, I suggested that in both of our interests, it might be better to seek someone else.

My social media presence changed, too. Instead of random pictures being posted every second day of me in some exclusive $1000-a-night suite wearing next to nothing, I preferred posting about issues closer to my heart such as sex worker law reform or issues relating to domestic violence – if I posted anything all. There's more than enough 'thirst trap' and humble bragging posts going around on social media as it is and God knows there are plenty of younger and fitter blokes out there who are more than happy to pick up where I left off.

But all that said, the ride is definitely not over. I have to believe that Mitch made an impact and that he can continue to do so – in whatever form or shape that may be.

Chapter 64 – Goodbye

If this was going to be goodbye, I wanted it to mean something.

I wanted to remind Sam about everything that happened over the time we were in each other's lives and I wanted to tell her that by choosing me at the very beginning, she changed the trajectory of my life forever. I wanted to thank her for connecting our souls and giving me the ability to feel emotions I never thought existed.

But any time I thought about 'reminding' Sam, I realised I was fighting a losing battle. As I slowly walked to her house on that gorgeous summer's day, I tried to focus on the little things. The dogs barking. The trams dinging. My own footsteps. I worried about how much the woman that I hadn't seen for so long had changed and I was nervous. Or perhaps 'scared' is more accurate. We'd all been cooped up in lockdown for months and were slowly adjusting to a few more freedoms, and her carers had passed on the message that she was happy to see me. I'd messaged the friend that chastised me, several times, practically begging to see her or to get any sort of update, but in the one lousy response I received, I was told Sam wasn't comfortable with that given how her disease had progressed. All I knew was that she was now only barely able to pour her own cereal and that the act of making a sandwich, or even finishing long sentences, was well beyond her. My heart stung when I read that she had begun to suffer from seizures and had nightmares so horrible that she shouted out to her full-time carers for comfort.

In my weaker moments, I'd think of her and the tears would just flow. I would inhale air and exhale tears. Crying became easy for me, which was a good thing, I suppose. The thought of seeing her, so much weaker, and so much less herself, and so incredibly vulnerable, was an utterly terrifying prospect for me but I had to do it. And finally, I'd been given one last chance.

Many years ago, I won a sales competition where the prize was a trip to Queenstown, New Zealand. I thought I'd give bungee jumping a try while I was there and many weeks before I did it, I visualised how I would overcome my fears. I decided the only way to find the courage to take that leap was to completely empty my mind, step forward and jump. Just bloody do it. Opening the door to Sam that day felt no different.

And then all of a sudden, there she was. And she looked small and frail. Her hair had grown well past her shoulders and was now greyer than ever. It wasn't particularly cold that day but she was wearing the same green jumper she always wore, as well as a woollen shawl, which was draped over her tiny shoulders and some very old-looking Ugg boots. She looked much older, but more than anything, she looked very, very tired. Constantly racking your brain to remember even the most basic things would wear anyone down, I imagine.

'Hey, Sam...' I managed.

I couldn't look her in the eyes and I had to time my words with my breaths, in a vain attempt not to cry. I took a tentative step towards her and opened my arms, almost instinctively. She slowly took a couple of robotic steps before she fell into me, and rested her head on my chest. The effect completely disarmed me. I lost my battle and sobbed as quietly as I could manage. I felt like I had to hold on to her even more tightly in an attempt to not lose all control.

'I've missed you, Dan. Everything's... shit.'

Her words were flat and emotionless, but hearing her speak my name flooded me with relief. She remembered my name. After a few minutes, I led her to the couch so we could sit some more and talk. As always, I was guided by her and would do whatever she wanted me to. I wanted to put my arm around her and just cuddle her back to how she once was but it didn't feel right. It wasn't my place to touch her anymore. All the sex, the laughter and the love we shared was in the past now – and in my memory only. So, I just gently held her hand as we sat. In silence.

If this was going to be goodbye, I thought, I didn't want anything to be awkward or forced because, even though she wouldn't remember it for long, I knew that I'd never forget that moment for as long as lived.

'I don't have much to say.'

She was staring blankly at my chest while she said it – in a manner that made me feel like she was talking to someone else.

'It's nice to see you again.'

I just kept trying to smile. Each breath seemed to cave my chest in further and further.

Twenty minutes passed while we sat – almost completely silent – just holding each other's hands. It didn't feel uncomfortable at all. In fact, it felt beautiful, because I realised that most of the reason she wasn't initiating any conversation was because that skill had dwindled away and not because she was uncomfortable. My previous research had already educated me about that aspect of the illness and how people became anxious about talking for fear they might say the wrong thing. It didn't matter to me. Silence doesn't have to be uncomfortable and when two people truly know each other and truly appreciate each other's company, simply sitting together without saying a word can feel as natural as breathing.

She didn't complain about anything, didn't mention her kids or say much at all, other than to tell me that she liked the way my hand felt on hers – and that I'd put on weight. I laughed and scootched closer, hoping for a hug, but in another room, a voice called out to her, asking her if she was thirsty.

'That's Kelly.' She said it with a lilt of surprise before she stood up and very slowly left the room.

I heard some murmurs from the kitchen. When she returned, Sam told me it was her carer asking if she was okay. Sam didn't seem bothered by the intrusion, but to me, it was a reality check. I realised that the last forty-five minutes or so was probably the longest length of time she'd been out of her carer's sight in a long time and it seemed my time was up. I told Sam how wonderful it was to have spent a peaceful afternoon with her, just sitting and holding her hand, and how happy it made me to see how well she was. The latter part was a lie, of course, but I figured she could do with a little positivity.

'Don't forget – you can call me or text me any time you like,' I offered.

I immediately cursed myself – 'Don't forget?' Choosing the right words is so hard sometimes. But in that situation were there any right words? It's difficult enough saying goodbye to someone under normal circumstances, but when that person has such a limited time left, it makes everything agonisingly real and incredibly hard to process. There literally are no words you can say to make things better.

My chest began to feel heavier than ever. I was going to cry, and I had to get out of there and into the privacy of my car. The only solace came in knowing that hopefully, Sam's lack of a short-term memory would spare her some of the sorrow that was already beginning to completely overwhelm me.

It'd been a long time since money had changed hands between us and I was glad. I didn't want my last memory of Sam to feel anything like a transaction. In many ways, however, this had been one of the most significant transactions of my life. In exchange for a small amount of my own time, I'd received a wonderful gift from an amazing woman who was coming to the end of an amazing life. She had chosen me to love and me to be loved by. It truly was an absolute honour. If I was able to remind her of that love – even if it was for just a few brief moments – then it felt like one of the most valuable things I'd ever done. What's meaningful is always different for different people, but at that moment, I believed that deep down, Sam loved me just as much in return. She would forget our story – I knew that – but I knew my memories of her would never fade.

I hoped that her young children would never forget her – as painful as that might be for them. And as a beautiful, sexual woman, I knew I'd keep my own memories of her safe and try to hold on to them for as long as I lived. I figured it was the least I could do, and sadly, all I could do.

Ours is not a sweet, romantic story, like *The Notebook*. It doesn't have a happy, satisfying ending – one that is neatly wrapped up before the credits roll. I'm still as fallible as always, but striving to be a better man with each new day. But this story was still a story of love. And it happened to us. Sam's full and exciting but sadly shortened life touched many people and created some wonderful memories – especially for me. And, despite all my flaws, my addictions, my anxieties and all my highs and lows, I want more than anything for Sam to know how much she inspired me, and that by bravely fighting her battle, she has forever inspired me to keep doing the same.

Afterword

As I lay here in my beautiful little apartment, my candles smelling as delicious as they do every night, I enjoy the sensation of silence gently vibrating in between my many thoughts. Melbourne being Melbourne, I can also smell the sweet, fat drops of rain she's once again blessed us with. It's in these quiet moments, when time doesn't seem to move and I feel at peace, that I often find my mind wandering. Fond memories of the past flow more easily now and I feel as though my inner critic – that internal and relentless voice prompting me to be better than the next guy – is slowly becoming just a tired and annoying whisper and not the vicious bully it once was.

Being a vulnerable man, I've come to realise, is not only okay – it's actually quite attractive. I feel comfortable in revealing that leaving the sex industry has been really, really hard for me. For the sake of closure, I've had to say goodbye to women I've known for years, loved wholeheartedly and will always achingly miss. It was never going to be easy, I knew, but the time finally came when I had to accept that I provided the best service I could, but part of that service required me to let go. I've tried many times to find out how Sam is, but sadly, I don't think I'll ever know. All I can do now is respect her privacy and hope that she is at peace. Helplessness, like regret, is a pointless and damaging emotion, so

I feel truly blessed for retaining a wonderful friendship with my ex-wife. We remain united as parents and stand ready to provide our little man with whatever he needs to learn to be kind and happy. My inevitable 'lows' continue to roll in and cloud my thinking from time to time, so I'm conscious of not burdening her when that happens. She's had enough of that. But it's in those moments of pain and self-doubt that I often wonder,

'Am I a good man?'

Mitch apparently was. People said he was kind and handsome and all sorts of other nice things, but what about the *real* me?

I often question whether I really did make a difference as people said, or whether I was merely a distraction. Was my purpose to simply delay people's pain? I guess that's an inner narrative for me to reconcile as time and life move on, and I hopefully gain some wisdom as I age.

I am now faced with being myself again and – this is the amazing thing – it doesn't feel quite so terrifying. My future remains uncertain – as I seem to like it – but my general path is now crystal clear to me. As Mitch and as Dan, I find myself in a very special position where I feel I can help guide and educate the next generation of men. And most importantly, my son. He needs me. It's time for me to be Daddy again.

Shawline Publishing Group Pty Ltd
www.shawlinepublishing.com.au

SHAWLINE
PUBLISHING
GROUP

More great Shawline titles can be found by scanning the QR code below.
New titles also available through Books@Home Pty Ltd.
Subscribe today at www.booksathome.com.au or scan the QR code below.